In Service to Love
Book 2: Love Elevated

In Service to Love
Book 2: Love Elevated

A Dynamic Experience of Consciousness,
Transformation, and Enlightenment

Darlene Green
Emissary of Love

Printed in the United States of America

First Printing, 2020

ISBN-13: 978-1-949003-64-2 print edition
ISBN-13: 978-1-949003-65-9 ebook edition

Waterside Productions
2055 Oxford Ave
Cardiff, CA 92007
www.waterside.com

To Love.

I allow Love's abundance to reign over me.
Ever present to blessings, I stand in the light of Love,
and say, "Yes!"
And so it is.

IN SERVICE TO LOVE

A Dynamic Experience of Consciousness, Transformation, and Enlightenment

In Service to Love Book 1: Love Remembered, Days 1–122
In Service to Love Book 2: Love Elevated, Days 123–244
In Service to Love Book 3: Love Now, Days 245–366

Visit the author online at
www.darlenegreenauthor.com or www.thedivineremembering.com.

When you watch flocks of birds crossing your evening sky, you will notice there are usually a few of the flock that are the leaders. They support the well-being of the whole flock by flying in a key position of leadership. There is no extra thought process that has them assume that role. They are fulfilling the unique qualities of their design. You too, are a leader of the flock. The inner yearning that is at the core of your being is not the active quality for most.

What is it that makes leaders different? Leaders of enlightenment move beyond the mastery of life to directing their attention to the mastery of being. You, as a leader of thought, seek the wisdom of your divinity. When others are looking outside for direction, you look inward and beyond consensus.

In Service to Love

TABLE OF CONTENTS

BOOK 2: LOVE ELEVATED

LOVE'S STAND

Love is not passive. Love invites you, urges you, to your greatest expression.
Available Now in this immaculate moment, Love meets you in the effort.
The direction of Love, through the myriad of expressions, is clear and precise.
Love is All there is. Love is All.

Your intention when you incarnated into your life was to be in service to Love,
through your perfect, unique expression.
Love is all you have ever wanted. Love has been what has driven your
soul's desires.
Through your own specific life events, you find yourself at this Now moment.
The urgency for the presence of Love rings ever louder within your soul as
you stave off the feelings of hopelessness that perhaps Love's voice is wan-
ing, or perhaps Love is losing the battle.

Love is here NOW!

The perceptions you have had of Love's vulnerability, of the fragility of
Love, are echoes of your past efforts to express Love within an environment
that did not honor or recognize Love's voice.
Those are echoes of a time gone by.
We urge you to release what you thought you knew of Love and be present Now!
Love is the force of creation!
Love honors, Love expands, Love naturally seeks full expression.
The evolutionary process you find yourself within now on the planet Earth is
Love seeking full expression of Love.

Rather than sinking into the mire of where Love is not, we support your courageous journey to you.
In Service to Love *reaches out to you, in support of you remembering what is already so of you.*
Who you are is a divine expression of Love.
Who you are is Source, extended into form.
Love asks you to make the stand for Love that Love makes for you.
Take on the personal responsibility of your own full expression.
Claim your divine essence Now. BE the contribution you chose to be.

We are in a unique station in the evolutionary process of creation. At the turning points of evolution, an opening exists that redefines what is possible.
The perceived problem is not sourced through the absence of Love.
The source of the planetary issues is a lack of responsibility.
When the experience of your external world continues to be advanced in technology that requires less and less of you to be present, there is a falling into the drugged world of "absence."
We send out the clarion call that would awaken you to your own divine and expansive truth!

When do you choose to no longer be enslaved by unconsciousness?
The harsh and unkind binds of the physical world are easily surmountable.
Take the hand of Love and see newly.
See beyond the clouded perceptions of collective consciousness. Hold a higher bar for yourself
and for the future of the planet Earth and beyond.
Trust Love. BE Love.

We incite you to action! Love is NOT passive!
Mobilize your highest expression. Mobilize your curiosity to find your own divinity.
Be open to the beauty around you and allow that to inspire you to see the beauty in yourself.
Self-worth is the main gateway through which you must pass.
Who you are is Source.

If you really believed that, what could be possible? What could no longer be possible?

Through the evolving, expanding expression of Love, we invite you to hold the courage to see the brilliance of your essential Self. When you hold a broad perspective, you lose the limitation of myopic density. Choose to rub the sleep from your eyes and wake to a new day!

Invite Love to take your hand, walk beside you, and reveal unto you the brilliance that resides within you Now!

LOVE
July 2019
Seattle, Washington

(You may view the YouTube video at:
https://youtu.be/hMBYrz-_pk4)

WELCOME

When humanity faces the most difficult of times,
it is innovative thought that opens the doors to possibility, ushering in a
new paradigm.

You are on the leading edge of an era that restores peace and wholeness
through the expansion of Love's light. You have always felt there is more.
You have recognized the veil of illusion as a limited perspective, leaving
absent the credibility of your essential Self. Our physical presence is only
part of our story.

Welcome to *In Service to Love Book 2: Love Elevated.* This is the second part of a three-book body of work totaling three hundred sixty-six days of writing. As I now look back at the process of writing with Masters for one year and one day I see the development of an exquisite process of enlightenment that is lovingly offered for my and your consideration. This book comprises entries for Day 123 through Day 244 carrying on where *In Service to Love Book 1: Love Remembered* left off. With many of the foundational concepts already introduced, this book continues with light, frequency, and messages to support the application of the concepts to your life. This is not meant to live as a philosophical discussion. No kidding. This is meant to make a difference in your life. It takes a certain tenacity to be willing to follow an inner calling that reaches awareness beyond the world we see—but you already knew that.

First, a few steps back to set the stage for what is to come. *In Service to Love* began with profound events on December 26, 2017. With invitation by Masters in light, I sat daily as Scribe, student, and member of the Council of Light for one year and one day. I have been guided through the limitations of my human nature to reveal my divine nature. In an experience that continues to expand my perspective I see consciousness, transformation, and enlightenment as a natural evolutionary step; as natural as transitioning from adolescent to adult. When our divine nature is no longer held separate, we may choose to claim our wholeness. If you can consider that who we are is Source extended into form; more of us resides in light than in form. One of the foundational concepts of this work is living the reality of our divine nature. As I sat with the Masters each day to write, I experienced the potent presence of Love inviting me to the farthest reaches of my awareness. With each discovery, I feel more and more like me.

Today, almost one year after the completion of *In Service to Love's* 366 Days, I still sit with the Council of Light daily. Their messages and frequencies guide me through an ever-evolving experience of living a life that is enlightened. I am drawn into deeper and finer realms of knowing, where each step anchors my divine nature and continues to true up an almost laser-like alignment with my I AM Self, valuing equally my divine nature and my human nature. With application in my life daily, the work of *In Service to Love* is a process of authenticity. A sacred gift available to all of us.

My experience of this extraordinary process is my wholeness. I see my Self live beyond the limitations I had previously thought were inviolable. I access the light of my divine essence as I follow the guidance of my I AM Self. As I lay claim to my wholeness on all levels of my being, my ecstatic joy in each moment is present always. I look at life through the lens of Love. I am touched by the beauty of All. From the perspective of my humanity I still have my moments of reaction, but I realize that is not my truth. I am able to shift my perspective with greater ease now. When my life is no longer clouded with perceptions of limitation, fear, and low self-value, I am able to shine, reaching the courage to be the contribution I intended as I planned this lifetime. Previously, shrouded with the fear of being seen, my thoughts of my Self for most of my life were, "But it's only me," and I lived below the radar of my life. As I choose to be the courage to move into an unknown realm, I follow my soul's deepest, sacred mandate of expression. I had suspected, and now know that our greatest innovations are available as we connect with our divine essence. Now, each day I step into my greatest expression.

Through my experience with *In Service to Love*, much of the mystery surrounding enlightenment is lifted. I see enlightenment as the reality that is possible with the alignment of our divine nature and our human nature. Rather than creating through the density of our humanity only, our divinity contributes at the very highest of frequencies, opening the door to our best life to be lived right now. What if the profound moments of your life were not just a fluke experience, but a peek into the eternal truth of you? What if you could consciously access the wisdom, inspiration, and innovation held naturally by your I AM Self? What if you could hear the clarity of your soul's voice beyond the limitations of your human nature? There is a treasure trove available within the choice for aligning with your highest truth.

Enlightenment is the process of uncovering our greatness as we lay claim to our wholeness.

As you accept the invitation of engaging with *In Service to Love*, which has been placed upon the sacred space of your altar, you too are met with the guidance and support of the Masters of the Council of Light. The ultimate truth of you is Love. The foundation of this extraordinary experience may only be Love. Within the potent field of Love, foundational concepts are offered for your consideration. With you at choice in each moment, your humanity is led to broader perspectives, beyond habit and the default ways of living, toward your unique truth discovered through resonance. This is a very personal and sacred path. If you are drawn to this work, I invite you to be present with the messages as they are specifically designed for you. Fine-tune your senses to feel the frequency that is present with each message; each day is different. Your multidimensional capacities are supported with rich frequency, light infusions, activations, meditations, and exercises.

Consciousness is the new frontier.

The experience of enlightenment is not the end. It is the beginning. What becomes possible through the wisdom of enlightenment is the point. What if the mission of your soul were fully expressed and you became the greatest contribution possible?

The fine frequency of your I AM Self offers transformation and innovation rather than change. If you are looking for your greatest innovative expression, look inside; you already are the treasure you seek. The only thing in your way is the limited perception of your human nature. Choose your wholeness where your human nature is fully integrated with your divine nature. In so doing, the frequency of your life increases beyond your wildest dreams, making possible the vision of your soul made manifest.

The chaotic world we live in is an opening that requires the best of us. We each came here with a mission, with an intention to be fulfilled. The transitional time we find ourselves within invites each of us to show up! The time is Now.

You are a leader on the edge of Love's evolution. It is with great reverence and Love I urge you on to your destiny fulfilled.

I remain,
In Service to Love,

Darlene Green
Seattle, Washington
December 2019

A Message from the Council of Light

You are invited to engage with your own divine process. The invitation rests upon the altar of your sacred space. As you choose a new perspective, to see what's possible, to see what you have not seen before, we are here. Love beckons. When you choose to accept the invitation upon your altar, we begin.

In Service to Love *addresses an imbalance in life experience. The collective consciousness that is pervasive is one that represents old ways of being. Much of the pain within the physical experience reflects the separation that exists in consciousness between who you are, your perceptions, and how you live. You are on the precipice of a new world. One that is in alignment with who you are as a divine expression of God.*

The purpose of our divine collaboration is to offer a new way of being that is in alignment with your innate divine expression and allows you to be in the physical experience in a way that is seamless. Meaning that you access all of you, beyond limitations, and live a life that is heart centered and soul centered. From the stance of your divine nature, you hold the light and Love that is you and bring your gifts and light to the world to be the unique expression of Love that you are.

The consciousness that drives many of the world's most visible imbalances at this time is grounded in division and separation. This applies to all areas of concern; the environment, politics, and humanitarian crises. In order to transform these issues, you are invited to move to a place where your best resides. Your best resides beyond your perceived limitations and the consciousness of past eras, in a new space that is inhabited only in the Now moment, where you have available the vision to create from your highest expression. You are already the answer. When you align with your highest expression, your frequency is naturally at a level that is authentic for you, you hold the light of Love, and your presence transforms. When you align with your divine truth, you hold space for collaboration of the highest form, which brings heaven to earth and opens new avenues of possibility and ways of being. You hold open the space of possibility that is divinely created. When you align with the limited frequency and consciousness that is the reflection of the problem, there can be nothing else possible beyond more of the same. As you choose the "more" that resides beyond what you already know, you access the vast expanse of your being and the light of possibility. The vibrating field of potential that is guided by the sacredness of being is catalyzed.

What can be possible as you align with your divine nature? Equally, what is no longer possible within the framework and pervasive presence of Love?

The challenge is to BE the courage that is willing to see beyond what is taken for granted, and then, through your inspired moments, to move into action and BE all that is for you to BE.

YOU are the light of the world. Now what?

We remain,
In Service to Love,
The Council of Light

About the Author

An innate empath, teacher, and healer, Darlene was aware of her Council as early as four years of age. Profound events and sensitivities revealed an ability to reach beyond the reality seen by most. Darlene found a home for her sensitivities as she began studying vibrational healing in 1992. She has written and led programs on living consciously, beginning in 1998 in Seattle, Washington. As a practitioner of Natural Force Healing and a Reiki master, she has utilized her intuitive gifts as a massage therapist practicing in clinical settings in Seattle from 1992 to 2012, when she left to answer a deeper calling. At sacred sites in Southern France, Darlene connected powerfully with her Council of Light and returned to her ancient heritage as Scribe. In 2015 Darlene was invited to create and host a radio program in Phoenix, Arizona, through VoiceAmerica's 7th Wave Channel, titled *The Inner Frontier,* the first step into a global reach. All external work ended as of a severe auto accident early in 2017 when focus turned deeply inward for healing.

On December 26, 2017, Darlene awoke to exalted spiritual events and an invitation by the Council of Light for divine collaboration in a body of work titled *In Service to Love.*

Darlene resides in Seattle with her husband, Ed Green, and their sweet golden retriever, Hailey Grace.

About the Council of Light
Composed of Masters, the Council of Light includes the voices of: Jesus, Mary Magdalene, Archangel Michael, Archangel Gabriel,

Melchizadek, Infinite Oneness, Isis, the Elohim, Buddha, Sanat Kumara, Metatron, the Hathors, Gaia, the Grandmothers, the Grandfathers, St. Germain, Legions of Light, and many more. The Council's presence is vast. The configuration shifts depending on the topic. Thoth, as "Patron of the Scribe" is the facilitator of frequency in light. The experience of the Council of Light is one of Love itself. Throughout the year of writing *In Service to Love*, the Council of Light evolves, from identification of individual masters to the singular voice of Love.

Appreciation

The gifts in my life are beyond counting. First, thank you to God, Source of All. Living the reality of my divinity is a sacred gift; a treasure beyond my ability to speak the words. Thank you, blessed Council of Light, for holding my hand and leading me to my truth throughout my life, to this collaboration of *In Service to Love*. It is hard for my humanity to comprehend the magnitude of what becomes possible with the exquisite experience of alliance with Masters of light, in light. I am in deep reverence and appreciation. Always.

From the vast perspective I now hold, I see the perfection of each step of my life, particularly when I wasn't conscious enough to dare entertain the audacity of my own divinity. Thank you, Love, for guiding me through the times when I couldn't see. I am deeply grateful for my family. Debbie, I asked God to not send me here alone, and I was given the gift of you; we hold an eternal bond of Love. Bonnie, I cherish our soul's connection more than I can say. A destiny of Love. Thank you, both, for your unwavering Love and support that encourages and blesses me daily. Shelley, you are treasured and always held close in my heart. I send Love and appreciation to our parents, grandparents, and lineage, all of whom have set the stage for the opportunities we hold dear now. Thank you, Mark B., Rob H., and Mark S., for your Love, friendship, and for cherishing my sisters.

Sean, Brandon, Cara, Bailey, Parker: If you could only have seen the Love and pride for you reflected in your grandparents' eyes.

And now you move on with your own lives and families, knowing you are Loved and supported by many who embrace our newest family members and those yet to arrive.

Kenny, Michelle, and Deb: Thank you for the precious gift you are. Always closely held in my heart, you are cherished for all you are and will become. Now it is a joy to watch you expand the voice of Love in your own families. Hanna, Colby, Braedon, and Mason; thank you for the contribution of Love you have always been. Your unique expression in the world is a treasure. May you find your voice and follow your heart.

I have had the honor of encounters with Masters in the physical realm, each brilliantly shining the light of Love that beckons me to my own truth. Thank you, Esther Hicks, Maureen St. Germain, Danielle Rama Hoffman, Sheila and Marcus Gillette.

I have been guided by synchronicity to Bill Gladstone of Waterside Productions Inc. Thank you for saying yes to *In Service to Love*. Thank you to all in the Waterside Productions family for your guidance and support. Frank Ferrante, thank you for your contribution to transformation. Thank you, Randall Libero, Senior Executive Producer of VoiceAmerica Talk Radio and TV, for your kindness and patience as I realized a global reach. Thank you, Fauzia Burke of FSB Associates, for holding the expansive vision of *In Service to Love*. Thank you, Jeanne Kreider, and Dave Kreider of Bellevue Wellness Center, and Kenneth Y. Davis, DC, and Lisa Davis, for your healing support, vision, and teaching.

So many people have contributed to me that it is impossible to name each person with the acknowledgment that fully recognizes the gift you are to me. I send Love and appreciation to each of you unnamed here but indelibly present in my heart. Thank you.

Dearest Lynn H., and Kristin W., thank you for your sacred sisterhood. You were the first ones I recognized in my soul tribe. Mary M., Terri G., Mary A., Jeff S., Laima Z., SandraAlyse W.: We have reunited through Danielle Rama Hoffman in answer to our unique, divine inner calling. I see the depth of vision, commitment, and light you hold. Thank you for being you, so I may see more of me.

KahMaRea M., you are a light I recognized immediately. Thank you for your Love and support. Your deep trust and devotion continue to inspire me. Bethany F., we have traveled a long way together, and each step is a gift. Thank you for your Love, support, and friendship. MaSanda G., thank you for your mastery and friendship. You emanate Love.

Thank you, Heather Clarke, Founder of Arizona Enlightenment Center, for holding the vision of enlightenment. Thank you, Maria Radloff, for your support and guidance. You are the best. Thank you, Joanne, of Joanne West Photography for your vision and brilliant light.

Thank you Ed G., Debbie B., Bonnie H., KahMaRea M., Kristin W., Katannya C., Michelle W., Mary M., Terri G., Mary A., Jeff S., Lynn H., Sheryl T., Heather C., Lynn L., Tresje S., Marcia P., and Mary R., for graciously receiving the daily words of *In Service to Love*.

Ed, every day is better than the last. My heart is filled with Love and appreciation for the gift you are. Our life together reflects the sacred journey of consciousness. We have always seen the divine light within each other. Thank you for your Love, support and passionate spirit.

In Love always,
Darlene

An Overview of This Work,
a Note from Darlene

In Service to Love is a divinely guided work where your unique process of enlightenment, conscious awareness, and realization of the exquisite divine expression of you is supported. With each day's gathering, you sit with me, Darlene, as your Scribe, and the diverse panel who make up the Council of Light, from the perspective of Love. Created in the Now immaculate moment, you follow the potent process of shifts in frequency and perspective that bring you the opportunity to move beyond barriers, revealing the unique expression that is your divine nature. This is a nonlinear process. Through concepts, analogies, and frequency, you move beyond your thinking into a resonant experience in which your own clarity is accessed.

Although this work will support your reach into the vast light expression of your true nature, we do not lose sight of the importance of then bringing that broader awareness into action in your day. The idea is to support you really living your best life right now. You do not have to spend lifetimes in the Himalayas in order to touch the divine of your essence. Finding your divine essence is not the end; it is the beginning. After the divine remembering is the divine remembered.

Not too far into the scribing, it became clear that the work of *In Service to Love* is communicated beyond words through an energetic presence of Love. This is a multidimensional body of work divinely orchestrated. The experience of Love is palpable.

You experience the evolution of this work with me. What becomes possible is a shift in perspective so complete that the potential exists to become unrecognizable to yourself from a consciousness point of view and, in the process, be so much more of who you are innately. This has certainly been my experience, and it continues to evolve. This is the ultimate expression of authenticity. From the integration of our human nature and our divine nature we access our divine birthright of joy, Love, peace, abundance, freedom, and more. When we release the entanglement of beliefs, habits, and collective consciousness, we discover the edges of our vast, divine essence in light. We can then learn to navigate our expansive capability and be informed by our soul.

The way to be with this work is to take each day on its own merits. I recommend being with the messages in the order they are written. However, in all instances follow your own inner guidance. Read only as much as you can absorb by being fully present. Try to sense the frequency that infuses the message. Each day is rich on its own. Bring your attention to your own fine-tuned awareness. Even though the messages from one day to another will expand on a concept, this is not a linear experience. The frequency and light of one day will be different from the next. Each day weaves a golden thread revealing your own truth. Even though you already hold the capability of movement in fine light realms, there is an aligning of your human nature with your divine nature that is occurring. This forms a broad base of integration for stability in your expansion and soul's work to come.

The Becoming of You

Every entry of *In Service to Love* reveals an energetic pathway for your own expanding awareness. As you raise your frequency, you are no longer mired in the density of your surroundings and yet see the beauty around you more acutely. As your perspective broadens you see more clearly your own perfect unique expression of Love. Not someone else's idea of you, or even your idea of who you "should" be. In releasing who you are not, you be-come. Enlightenment is the becoming of you. This is not a passive process. When you take the topic of spirituality beyond an inspiring moment or experience you are left with the prospect of shifting your reality.

Understand who you are is already perfection, with nothing added and nothing taken away. Our conversations are not about changing you. Our conversations are about championing the reason why you came to Earth in the first place. Consider that there has been not one misstep, not one event or moment that has not been perfect in your experience. Each step has taken you to the potent moment of Now where what you have always known becomes possible. Every step of your life is to be appreciated as your soul moves into the phase of becoming. The state of "become" is the full alignment of your conscious awareness with your divine essence, with Source. From this vast perspective, you see why you are here.

A Note of Responsibility

When you allow your Self to follow your unique process of enlightenment your view of reality will change, as it must. This work is a catalyst for a shift in the experience of reality that engages your divine nature. At times the process is disorienting to your human nature as you find your next steps. While you are experiencing a pull to your greatest expression, and before you jump into transformation, we take this moment to address responsibility.

The veil of illusion for all the negative connotation also holds comfort and a perception of safety, not to be taken lightly. While you access your greatest Self please become aware of ways you already conceal truth to yourself. If you are utilizing a substance that already alters reality, please reconsider. In the presence of addiction the experience of non-linear reality is destabilizing. The vast space revealed in this process requires a solid base of grounded presence. It has been my experience that even the most subtle ways I have denied my own divine essence come to the forefront inviting another choice. As I continue to say yes to my own divine journey, I have released ways of being that are not in my highest good. Knowing my thoughts create, discipline with my thinking is paramount. My food choices are cleaner, I rarely drink alcohol, I work out regularly and spend time in nature. As my perspective and energetic reach expand, my solid and balanced presence in the physical realm is required. By the way, I am also happier than I have ever thought possible.

Please take conscious responsibility for your choices. There are meditations, exercises, light infusions and divine support for you in this amazing process. And if your life choices are contrary to what you say you want, your lower frequency choices will win out, because you are the master creator in your life. As I have been told throughout this process by the Council of Light, "Darlene there is no magic wand that we hit you over the head with and bestow your divinity. You already ARE. We hold the mirror so you may see your own magnificence and mastery." So, for me, this is a process of taking responsibility and stepping-up in a big way to who I AM.

I live on the edge of what I know and what I don't know allowing my greatest wisdom space to engage. It takes something. You already hold the wisdom for yourself as well. This part of the work holds tremendous transformative potential. If you can hold the reality of transformation as a background perspective, gently allow your own divine nature to support your next steps and bring into form your greatest inspiration. (Where else could you find original thought?) Who you are is extraordinary. I am honored to be in your presence on the leading edge of Love's expression.

Take care of yourself and Love the people around you.

Darlene Green

February 1, 2020

Love's Invitation December 2017

"Sit with us each day for a year and a day." The words spun through my being as I awoke on December 26, 2017. "Three hundred sixty-six days." I felt a presence surrounding me and through me at the same time. It was rich, deep, expansive, compassionate, potent, and clear. I was in the presence of Love! An experience of the profound and a return to home at the same time! Blessed! My head spinning, my personality perplexed, and my soul celebrating, I sensed a gathering of the highest order. I felt Thoth, Jesus, Mary Magdalene, Melchizadek, Archangel Michael, Archangel Gabriel, Legions of Light, the Elohim, and a vast sea of beings of light too brilliant to count. All were familiar and beloved. As I tried to settle into the experience, I sobbed in recognition of the answer to my deepest yearnings, which I'd so sacredly held that I didn't dare even utter them. Gently held within the experience of Love's rapture, I sat down at my computer. The words poured from my fingertips, and Day 1 began.

This is not about a privileged experience, only available to those few who are sensitive enough to hear. My sensitivity only turns up the volume so you may hear your own voice. It is about each of us living up to the promise of the life we had intended before we came here. It is easy to hold this work in the ethers and view it as separate from the exquisite moments of our day, as we get down to the business of living a physical reality. Instead, what this body of work offers is a connection to the divine perfection of you, brought to bear in life. What if you really knew what your purpose was? It is not a one-size-fits-all experience. This is about you and me each acknowledging our divine origin and bringing that knowing into our day to create the life that is ours to have in a way that makes a difference. In a way that allows us to live from our soul's purpose and be the contribution we have always known that we are. Our best life. My expression is unique, as is yours. What I have learned since the first day of divine collaboration with the Masters in light is the beauty of each of us. Irreplaceable, beloved, masterful, each with our heart's calling. We are being called to the brilliance of our own mastery. *"Beloved, remember who you are."*

This shift in awareness is offered through a divinely crafted experience of rich frequency that resides behind the words and is the catalyst for my unique process (and yours), led by our own divine guidance. In the process we connect with broader perspectives and begin to see behind the veil of illusion.

As a student of this process, I have traveled the formless realms of frequency, guided by the Masters, and realized my capacity for finely tuned awareness. I have not only scribed each day's writing, I have lived it, and it continues. The work was not delivered on a silver platter. With each day's lesson, I was gently invited to stretch what I knew possible, finding my own way and making choices from the larger, more vast perspectives that became clear. When I choose to take ownership of my authentic nature, I realize that what I have always been good at is being me. Difficulties and pain have occurred in my life when I strayed, trying to fit into what was "normal" or trying to numb the extraordinary sensitivity that is my true nature. I experience my greatest joy being all of me. Not just from the personality standpoint, but most importantly from the perspective of my soul. It is then that I truly honor my Self, and I then have the capacity to see your perfection too.

When I view life from the perspective of my own unique expression at its finest, I take ownership of the rich heritage of being Scribe. I am profoundly transformed. There is no longer a chasm between who I AM and who I BE. The work now is what becomes possible when what I have always sought is found. Now I do the sacred work of my soul. I AM a Scribe. I translate light and consciousness into form through words, both written and spoken. With who I am not, no longer a distraction, my frequency shifts as what I create is in alignment with my highest expression. You see, as I be more of the divine expression of me, I hold space for you to realize the divine expression of you. What becomes possible when we hold the perspective of our own divinity and our highest potential is realized? When we are in conscious collaboration with the divine, what is no longer possible? What becomes possible when Love is the lens through which we view all?

Day 123: Know Us Now

Good day. It is I, Thoth, stepping to the forefront of this divine conversation taking place within this Now immaculate moment. It is a new day! A new chapter opens before you. In Book 1 of *In Service to Love: Love Remembered,* the ground is prepared for shifts in awareness that reveal your divine nature. Your expanding awareness naturally shines light on barriers and limitations held unconsciously. In each moment you may make a new choice. *In Service to Love* is sourced from a foundation of Love that beckons your awareness to seeing beyond the limitations of your human nature to the broadest perspective that is informed by your divine nature. Then, in each moment, you choose from an empowered stance that which resonates with the truth of your being. The result is a reality that is in alignment with your highest expression, and the vision of your soul is moved from potential to actualization.

From the potent perspective of observer, resonance becomes the beacon that guides your choices. Your elevated perspective holds the door open to further refining your awareness, revealing yet more of your divine nature. The result is an experience of your wholeness. A feeling of Love, compassion, connection, and of being at home enhances life. The enlightenment process does not utilize anything beyond you.

Again, your Scribe reaches for her radical faith as we move forward. Consider that from the perspective of your human nature, the grandest possibilities of your divine design may not be seen. Through this divine collaboration, the potential exists for a shift in conscious awareness that sees, knows, and chooses to manifest your own unique divine design. Your knowing will keep you informed while the thinking catches up. We invite you to hold the perspective of your divine nature where you may stand beyond the limitations of your human nature.

Present as we move forward is a panel of light beings that are progressively vast and diverse, and includes those unique to your personal Council of Light. The space we hold today is for you to connect easily with the members of your Council of Light. They have always been present with you, as was part of your agreement from the onset of your lifetime. Some you may remember, see, hear, or sense. We invite you to a renewed connection to the highest level of divine support that surrounds you.

Intention for Our Next Steps Together

We request you write down on a piece of paper your intention for this next level of work together within In Service to Love. *As you hold the intention of BEING Love and then overlay your intention throughout your day, you are in creative territory. Remember, your BEING creates. Ask for clarity and allow the response to arise in your awareness.*

Rest in the knowing that it is possible to be in collaboration with Masters. Many works have been written through and by the Masters over eons. Your opus awaits. We invite you to know us now. We are here. We hear you. We remain, *In Service to Love.*

In Love,
With Love,
From Love,
The Council of Light

DAY 124: TEMPLATES OF LIGHT; ALIGNING WITH YOUR I AM SELF

As you reach into the light of your being, an integrating process must occur to accommodate your expanding perception. Often the work of enlightenment is perceived as something that is far away and difficult to attain. That would be true if you made no movement toward it or the process of enlightenment and conscious awareness made no move toward the you in form. Enlightenment is not a passive process, for sure. Within your intention to be present with the support of *In Service to Love*, both actions are taking place at one time. As you intend to integrate your divine nature and your human nature, your natural multidimensional awareness is activated. In Book 2 of *In Service to Love: Love Elevated*, we explore that capability a bit more. In Book 1: *Love Remembered*, we asked you to consider moving from the reality you held as default to consider other possibilities. We ask you to look yet again, beyond the boundaries of your perception to the unknown of possibility.

As you continue to make shifts in perspective, the steps all line up, and one step is a natural progression to the next and the next and the next. In the same way, you have been experiencing a lightening, an ease and freedom in your life, and the process continues as you experience your wholeness. You are reclaiming consciously what is already present as a part of your divine expression. Now, through your expanding awareness, consider that you are supplying less resistance to the experience of your authentic nature.

Today we ask you to consider the other-dimensional aspects of you. Within your divine design, like a blueprint, is the template for the highest expression of you mentally, emotionally, physically, and spiritually. This potential is held in light. As you access more of your divine nature, you move into alignment with your divine potential.

We know that words at this point go only so far in being a catalyst for your expansive process. The experiences must be felt, known, and processed through your internal resonance. As you declare your intentions for your next steps of enlightenment, the moments of your life become the canvas for your creation.

Your Template of Light

The purpose of this exercise is to explore the subtleties within the fine frequencies of your awareness and access the light of your divine nature as a contribution to your physical well-being. Consider that this exercise is not designed to fix you, as you are not broken. Its purpose is to support your reach into the fine light of you and see how your natural access to light supports all levels of your physical experience. Focusing on your wholeness, this exercise is one that will facilitate your access to your multidimensional expression.

Sit down, be comfortable, allow. Take a deep breath and begin to still your thoughts. Allowing them to fall around you, like spring's petals moving through a breeze.

You have many realities. Visualize before you your own mirror image, standing before you. Move to a place of stillness and Be.

Intend to see your totality. You are both form and light. You are Source extended into form. Feel the unseen and potent expression of you that resides in light. Your light expression holds your I AM Self. Feel yourself move to wholeness as you consciously integrate the light of your divine nature with the denser expression of you in form. Your light matrix holds the divine template of you. It holds within it your highest expression available in alignment with your I AM perfection.

Your state of perfection is beyond history, beyond life events; it is the design of you before your beliefs kicked in. Feel the vitality, the perfection of each cell as it vibrates with the manna of divine light. Feel the electrical field that has you connected naturally to all aspects of your light expression right here right now. Feel the magnitude of your totality. Sense the expanse of your Self. Feel the movement of fine frequency; you are expansive, brilliant, and charged with Love.

Notice the natural alignment of yourself in light and in form. You are always informed by Love. Love enlivens every cell of your body with divine vitality and information. Feel the electrical charge within your body alter slightly. Both peaceful and alert, you are aligning with your divine nature, with Love.

Who I AM is Love.
I align with my divine nature, and every aspect of my life honors the unique expression of Love that I AM.
I choose the highest expression of well-being in all areas of my life, led by my I AM Self.
Areas of resistance are now released with ease and grace as I integrate the fine frequencies of my divine light.
I integrate effortlessly with the essence of my Self held in light. I integrate perfectly with ease and grace for all my systems.

Within this exercise and those to come, you fine-tune your awareness. There is a type of linear perception that you have utilized in the past that identifies things, like a tree, desk, building, chair, pen. Now your awareness shifts to noticing equally both things and the space between things. You begin to fine-tune your nonlinear perception and pick up subtle cues. For example, imagine the colors of the rainbow. The colors before you are not all the frequencies that exist. Frequencies exist both below and above the range demonstrated in a rainbow's colors. Just because something may not be identified by normal vision, that doesn't mean it does not exist. Imagine your sensitivities fine-tuning to the point where they begin to see newly. Subtle shifts, imperceptible previously, now move onto your radar screen.

Day 125: Conversations of Light

As you have continued to uncover the barriers to your highest divine expression, your new "baseline" of being has increased in frequency. Do you notice your reality has shifted in the presence of high frequency and you are adept at recognizing the frequency you are within? You hold the ability to shift your way of being because you choose to. When your being shifts from an automatic or unconscious expression to a conscious choice, the light you access within your divine expression is catalyzed. More of the light that you are begets more of the light you are.

You recognize that the reality that is possible as you BE the frequency of a "problem," is only more of the problem. When you choose to alter your reality by creating from a more empowered, high-frequency way of being, you see the result almost immediately in your reality. Your perspective expands when you choose a new perspective. Possibility opens as you are conscious of your choices. The fluidity of creation is felt, and confidence is gained as you continue to take responsibility and create from your broadest, most expansive expression.

As you choose to be empowered in your choices, you are being informed less by the limitations of your personality and more by the expansive awareness of your divine nature. The light reality of you responds, opening new pathways of awareness.

When just the smallest amount of divine light is introduced, the door is opened to more. For example: We have just shifted from the evolutionary condition of separation consciousness to unity consciousness. It is not that the full-on expression of unity consciousness is anchored in all beings. Unity consciousness is now available. At one millionth of a second after midnight it is a new day. And the day is yet to be lived. The possibility of unity consciousness opened at the millisecond after the shift to unity consciousness became available in 2012. So it is with access to the you in light. At the smallest opening of light, all the light you are becomes available within the new realm that has opened. Perhaps not all actualized— but available. These are the conversations you have with the you in light.

And then of course, there are the conversations in light that are had with beings in light. Light holds a full, rich depth of vitality, wisdom, creation, divine expression, and Love. So much to be explored.

DAY 126: FAITH, DOUBT, TRUST, DIVINE KNOWING

As your awareness expands, the process of integrating is the space where you hold in your hands all realities. You sift and sort through information and experience to identify the resonance that is a fit for you in the moment. At this point it is helpful to identify the distinctions of doubt, faith, trust, and divine nature.

Your human nature needs categorization to get a handle on the nonlinear process of an expanding conscious awareness. Human nature requires "knowing" in order to secure safety. Remember, you are not leaving your human nature behind to experience divine nature, you are claiming your divine nature to express your wholeness. For example, this morning your Scribe Darlene was doubting her ability to move forward with this divine work. She was questioning the process in light that is occurring, wanting to be responsible for the work she has committed to. Our immediate words to her, and to you are, "Doubt is human nature, not divine nature." Once acknowledged, the doubt may be appreciated. Doubt is a process of active evaluation. In the space of doubt, conclusions have not been drawn. The options are held in view, allowing a new, more expansive picture to be revealed. Doubt evaluates options.

Faith moves past doubt into an open space of the unknown. It is faith initially that has you move beyond the spaces of your known world. Faith is employed at certain stages where the pieces don't seem to line up but you trust yet again.

Trust is the connection with the resonant inner voice that says, "All is well."

Your divine knowing holds the point of crystal clarity. Evidence is not needed within the frequency of divine knowing. You are informed by your highest Self. Within divine knowing is an anchoring into All.

We are in a background of unity consciousness. The background of creation is no longer oppositional as was the case with separation consciousness. Unity consciousness is all about wholeness and a claiming of your totality. As you hold your human nature in a space of wholeness and in communication with your divine nature, you integrate more easily that which is newly being revealed.

As you access more of the divine expression of you from the highest frequencies of your reach, you find that doubt, trust, and faith are not issues. You are living within a space of All, from your I AM. Your I AM presence does not question and evaluate. Your I AM chooses.

As the qualities of human nature are held in appreciation, the space opens to move past perceived limitations. The fact is you are currently human. Like the tiles of an exquisite mosaic, the expressions of both human nature and your divine nature create the totality of you.

DAY 127: EVERY DAY EXTRAORDINARY

This is not a journey of one step or even a few thousand. This is a journey of eons and of moments. The message today is one of appreciating the moments. In receiving this information daily, it is easy to move this to a part of your day that is habit. We would ask you to consider your stance. The work you are doing as you focus on the extraordinary during your day is making an impact not only with you but within your environment and those around you. Sometimes you may be tired, and you may be distracted with other areas of your life needing your attention. We remind you, however, that the work you are doing is extraordinary. Who you are is magnificence.

Today we stand in Love and appreciation for who it is that you are. Who do you have to be to undertake a journey most don't even see? We see you and hold you gently in Love.

We bathe you in the light of rejuvenation, supporting and sustaining your efforts to see and Be newly.

Sweet Dreams.

DAY 128: THE BEAUTY OF RESOLUTION

The conversation of enlightenment is distinct from the reality of living enlightenment and expanding awareness within the material world.

As you gradually shift the perspective that you have known of yourself to reveal new facets of your expression, there is an excitement as the increasing resonance indicates an alignment with your I AM Self. This resonant knowing often feels like remembering, and it fuels further exploration in that direction. We are utilizing the analogy of the faceted diamond to represent your totality. As you hold the diamond containing your greatest potential, what is first revealed is conscious awareness of your habits, beliefs, and actions within relationship to the present moment. In holding a stance of inquiry, you gain clarity and you see the benefits and barriers to your belief systems. You see those beliefs that have supported and propelled your expansion and you see those that seemingly have the weight of the world attached to them. The weighted issues represent those areas of your soul growth that are "ripe" for clarity. In some areas of life, your growth is easy and seems to rocket into expansion. Other areas may hold a level of resignation or a sense of being immovable. Today we communicate that the expansion of you does not fall along the lines of equal growth. Parts of you will move farther and faster than others. At some point as you behold the faceted diamond reflecting your brilliance, you must shift your position of the diamond to see the facets that were once hidden.

Resolution is an action of your being that evaluates all issues at hand and supports the equalizing of your growth. You have found parts of your awareness that have skyrocketed, and other parts, especially the "old" issues, are coming up for review. They surface as a process of resolution to accommodate the amount of light that is now present and available. Your openness reveals possibility. Possibility offers new choice, made consciously from inner reference and resonance. In the presence of your increasing light, you will experience resistance for old ways of being that are no longer a match. Arguments you have made in the past will come to the forefront of your awareness for reevaluation. It isn't that you need to work everything out; this is mostly a subconscious activity. These issues are coming up because the inner, higher expression of you is finding equilibrium.

The action of resolution is initiated from the intentions you hold and have declared. The parts of you that are not in alignment with your declarations will come up to be addressed. Within the background of unity consciousness, ideas and thought forms based in opposition no longer have "legs" to stand on.

The physical experience of resolution is not always comfortable. It is the experience of resistance. Your highest expression is at work adjusting the facets of your awareness. Know that in those moments, you have the beauty of resolution working for you. You are in process for the actualization of your highest expression. Those ways of being or situations that no longer resonate with you are requesting an infusion of clarity. Trust that there is an automatic component of this work. It often feels like deep work. Often your dreams will be active. The experience may feel unsettling. Ask yourself, "What part of me is feeling unsettled?"

The appearance of resolution is an indicator that your expansion is actively underway. Declare who you BE. Follow your resonance. Take care of yourself in those days. Meditate. Be the Love that you are to the best of your ability. Be clarity, Be grace, Be beauty, as you choose, and your intentions will support your move through to an empowered perspective on a large scale.

When the goal is being MORE of you, by definition, the parts that are not you will fall away. Resolution supports that process.

We hold an infusion of light that supports clarity, ease, and grace for your ongoing resolution.

DAY 129: BEING NEW

The process of the enlightenment shines light upon the distinctions of your being that are rooted in your human nature and your divine nature. In the same way there are basic needs that define and can predict human behavior, there are also ego and thought patterns that contribute some predictable characteristics. As you expand your conscious awareness to include the light expression of you, you embrace the vast range of the most linear to the most nonlinear aspects of you. That's a lot of information. Your human nature revels in a level of "known" that exists in your world. As you consider taking on your divine nature as well, there is a re-sorting and reconfiguration that must take place. The human ego and mind need to know, understand, and categorize to determine safety and proprioception, or place, in the environment.

As you understand the process of conscious expansion you may begin the sorting process that allows space for a new reality to show up. There has been enough of a shift to this point that these issues are beginning to rise in your awareness. We are in no way suggesting you ignore the patterns of your human nature in favor of the expression of you that resides in light. In fact, quite the opposite. This is a process of wholeness. There is a joining of all parts of you to allow the highest expression of you available to be accessed. It requires *all* of you, not just the parts your mind feels are worthy. This is the reason we move in small increments, allowing time and space for gradual shifts in perspective.

You as a human being will always lean toward the known, toward fact. We have had many conversations around the difference between the known world and the larger reality of you that is yet unknown. It is the edge of this inquiry of known and unknown that supports your presence in the Now immaculate moment. It is only within the Now moment that you find your highest expression available. So we have employed a variety of ways to get there: intention, declaration of being on a daily basis, meditation, breathing, light infusions, energetic support for integration and clarity, and other methods. As the need to know is supported, safety is experienced that also opens the doors gradually to the what-is-next.

One way you may see your inner dance with the known is through your ability to stay present. Both the past and the future are informed by parts of you that do not reside in the present moment. Are you feeling more weighted lately? Is the excitement of discovery waning a bit? Are you feeling out of touch with your extraordinary expression? Chances are good that you are not occupying the present moment in the same way as when we first began our journey together. By lending compassionate awareness to the process required to accommodate new information, you hold the key to gentle expansion.

This is a process of expansion done in a new way. As you bring all parts of you together, no part of you is sacrificed in favor of another part of you. At the core of the process of your conscious expansion is the understanding, remembering and realization of your divinity. Right here and right Now. You already have it All. You are All. We use the new ways of thinking and support new perspectives so you may begin to see what is already present.

The symphony of you has been played and heard throughout the celestial realms for eons. Each note holds perfection.

Be human. Be gentle. Be compassionate. Be divine. Be Love.

DAY 130: FOOTSTEPS OVER THE THRESHOLD

Today we acknowledge the multidimensional aspects of you that exist in a new way. You are a multidimensional being. Your days may feel like they are within one reality; but you occupy many places at one time as a being of light. These expressions in light hold the information that continues to beckon you almost magnetically toward your highest expression. You are more than the you seen in the mirror. You have many reflections. Like the diamond, there are many facets of your expression, some of them hold form and many do not. The light expression of you continues to infuse your physical being with light so that the days of your awareness are pulled forward one footstep at a time, toward the unhindered connection with your divine essence.

This may feel like a day that is much like many others, when in fact this very moment is a critical moment in your expansion. You choose on a moment to moment basis what to create. You have taken many steps forward with the intention to actualize the full expression of you. You have begun a process of conscious expansion, and now you are at the gateway of your expansion where another choice is appropriate. The choice at this moment of your expansion is to realign your inner world and your outer world so that the two coalesce into the highest expression of you. The result is a higher frequency expression of you that unlocks codes of knowing that are held within your divine light design. Available is the satisfaction and knowing of you as cohesive, potent, clear, and a divine expression of Love.

So, on one hand, this day is like many. From a larger perspective this is a pivotal moment. What is called for at this moment is your choice. The difference between the choice made today and the choices on other days is the space you inhabit as you make your choice. You are at a gateway or threshold of your next expression. A potent moment for choice.

Many are gathered in light here today in witness to your choice. The opportunity at hand is pivoting into the next stage of awareness that is perfect for you. The sense is of having outgrown your previous space of awareness, so a new space opens. Your choice is honored and supported through the divine collaboration of this work. The dynamic of collaboration will meet you where you are.

We acknowledge a pivot that is present at this moment for expansion, like a giant leap forward into the natural expression of you. There is opportunity available to move the potential into actuality.

Footsteps Over the Threshold

If you say yes to the opportunity at hand of specific and committed expansion of conscious awareness, we support your choice.

Move to a place of inner stillness. Visualize before you a door. Feel the familiarity of space you occupy before crossing the threshold. It is well known, and you have mastered many levels so far. In the same way a child moves from walking to running, you may choose to cross the threshold of access into your next higher expression of conscious awareness.

Your footsteps on the other side of the threshold are experienced with the clarity and purpose that comes from a deep wisdom you have always held. You are guided by you, as you venture into the next expression of you that is waiting. An expression that has been waiting for lifetimes in some cases. Familiar, expansive, natural, and possessing a high vitality. You have been preparing this space for you for some time. Welcome home.

With delight we meet you where you are and support your unique process of conscious awareness. The divine expression of you is breathtaking. You should see you from here. You shine brighter than a thousand suns.

DAY 131: CHOICE AND COMMITMENT

As we move to the point of choice, as in yesterday's transmission there is a door that is opened that holds you in the immaculate Now moment. When you experience a resonance, you gather all parts of you to the Now moment in order to make, as in the case of yesterday's opportunity, a choice. The transmission yesterday held within it the frequency that identified it as something different. The frequency was a resonant note. It was not a day of choosing vanilla ice cream or a turkey sandwich. There was a frequency resonance that communicated to you yesterday that this is something to consider. Regardless of your ultimate choice, the request for choice opened a door into the present moment for you. Could you feel it? What about yesterday's transmission piqued your attention? Perhaps it didn't. That is good to note, too.

At a choice point, a choice is made, period. The choice is to engage, agree, disagree, or something in between. Even a neutral or apathetic response is a choice. Once a choice is made, what generates the next step? We would like you to consider that your commitment does this.

The energy of you is focused and gathered around a commitment that follows choice. It is your commitment that generates a field for possibility. Your commitment holds the door open to the present moment by staying connected to the original choice and yet casts energy that supports a matrix of possibility that affirms the choice and sets the tone for the outcome. In demonstration, the process of choice and commitment provide fuel for the ever-expanding being of *In Service to Love.* An energy field or matrix that is multidimensional and held in a very high frequency surrounds *In Service to Love.* You may feel the support as being gently guided, as additional clarity, ease, being buoyed by your divine connection. At Day 1, Darlene chose this collaboration. In those initial moments, she was willing to meet the inner resonance in the Now immaculate moment, even though she had no idea what the completed product would be or how it would happen. She employed her radical faith in response to the deep resonance that prompted her choice. Once the choice was made, with every action, thought, and emotion around the deep resonance that was experienced by Darlene, her commitment followed the choice and the answer "Yes!" The matrix was then moved from potential to actualization. With continued commitment, the matrix continues to broaden and deepen exponentially.

Darlene uses the analogy of being pregnant with this work or being the chalice for this work. Once the divine design is received through choice, there is a developmental process that is underway that brings this work into form. It happens every day as Darlene sits at her computer with us, and it happens with momentum and now velocity. Your Scribe recognized a body of work that was in alignment with her highest expression when it was in front of her and she said, "Yes!" The "Yes!" fuels her commitment daily. Connecting with us and *In Service to Love* is held in a space now not only of commitment but with accelerating velocity of growth and expansion. The opening is created as Darlene continues to step into the Now moment and brings more of her authentic expression present.

The potential you hold is beyond your wildest imaginings. Moving from choice to actualization requires and mandates commitment. Commitment is the fuel that brings all your energy into focus and commitment is what manifests. This is a part of Manifestation 101. Who you are is a master creator. What are you creating? What are you committed to? Where is your energy and attention focused?

We ask you to consider being committed to your highest expression made manifest here and Now. That is an intention that is worthy of you. This journey is like no other. No suspense novel could hold the twists, turns and surprises that are in store for you with your choice and commitment.

Our Love, appreciation, and gratitude for you is beyond understanding.

Remember to laugh. Knock, knock.

DAY 132: RESONANCE NOW

G ood day. This is Infinite Oneness stepping to the forefront of this divine conversation today. As Infinite Oneness, I hold the collective of Love. From the collective, I speak of choice, resonance, commitment, and action as the process from which to manifest.

In the way you look at a tree most often, you see a tree. With closer inspection you see layers upon layers of information. You may see the individual qualities of the tree, such as the bark and its texture, the branches, shape, height, color, fragrance, energy, vitality, flowers, rings of the trunk, roots, depth, age, and on and on. The tree analogy applies to the depth and expanse of the mechanics surrounding creation and manifestation. There are many, many, layers that apply, each holding truth. When you look at one layer of observation it is true, and then, upon closer examination, a whole new world is revealed. As a scientist looks at cells and finds the empty space that is rich with information and potential, much exists between thought, resonance, and the creative process.

Resonance informs choice. It is the catalyst for a choice. Resonance also holds the fuel for the completion, or the charge that explodes the resonance into the next step of form. The charge occurs as the resonance of the idea or thought aligns with your essential truth, like magnets drawn powerfully together. In the aligning of the two there is a synergistic expansion, a colliding if you will, of creative forces. Resonance is the stuff that supports an aligning or direction of creation.

What is it that has you choose one thing over another? We assert that it is not a thought, it is resonance. Much like the frequencies of a rainbow, some of which are seen and many of which are beyond your visual ability, so too are the many levels of resonance. When you feel an internal resonance, it does not always get experienced as goose bumps. As you stand in the present moment, the more closely aligned you are with your divine nature, the stronger the resonance "signals" tend to be.

We would like to create a visual picture for you of the process of creation. Visualize a target on the wall for darts. Concentric circles ever widening around a singular point in the center-most location. We would like you to consider the center-most point to be the immaculate Now moment at the spark of creation. Intensity, clarity, power, and velocity is the greatest at the center point. Creation from this point is powerful, of high frequency, clear, aligned, multidimensional, holographic, dynamic, living, and evolving.

As you create farther from the center point, or from a point of less resonance, greater resistance is experienced. Like a hose that has a kink, the flow is not direct or powerful. If you look back in your life you can find times when the low resonance, lower-frequency choice is often like a firecracker that fizzles. It is helpful to know that the quality of the creations predictably reflects the frequency present at their inception.

As your thought, intentions, and choices are in alignment with the clarity of your I AM Self, they hold tremendous resonance, high frequency, and creative potency. As in the preparing of your evening meal, the quality of your meal is equal to the quality of the ingredients and preparation. The quality and nature of the components of creation inform the quality of the outcome. All this is directed by the level of resonance and choice. Resonance, like divine design, requires a chalice or canvas and clear action that moves the inspiration into form. Otherwise the resonance is a great idea and is gone one moment later. Resonance informs choice, then the creative dynamic is accelerated into the manifestation process, requiring action.

Following choice is the commitment and action that continues the creative cycle. With each thought, emotion, and action in alignment with your choice, you will find that the resonance will also continue to evolve and grow and continue to ask for choice, commitment, and action.

We bring this up today to point out the incredibly powerful dynamic that is universal law. It has been, is, and always will be part of the dynamic of creation. From the background of separation consciousness, where opposition and conflict reigned, resonance also held a restraint of sorts. With the background now of unity consciousness, creation is accelerated with your choice and commitment to wholeness.

What level of resonance are you experiencing? Like the pedaling of a bicycle that propels forward motion, do you see how the continued alignment with resonance, choice, and action begets more resonance, choice, and action? Do you see how as you connect with the highest frequency resonance at the Now immaculate moment, you are aligning at a high level, and the result is almost laser-like?

How can you reach that which is your divine work? There are many ways. Continue to shed that which is not you, and your moments spent in the divine immaculate Now moment will increase. You have already experienced those moments. Rather than a momentary experience, resonance is a beautiful access to your divine creative process.

We invite you to align newly with resonance. Resonance is your I AM Self communicating through your human nature. As you follow the light of resonance you align with your greatest expression.

A whole new realm has opened as you reach more deeply into the light expression of you.

Day 133: Your Expansive Nature Resides Beyond Words

Enlightenment is a natural evolutionary process in realization and actualization of your divine nature. What makes this process so unique is the step-by-step movement that supports your conscious awareness along the way. You see, you already are the divine being you are. That doesn't change. What shifts in this process is your conscious realization of your truth. No one else's truth: yours. This process could be likened to a tour abroad. Your accommodations, meals, and activities are prearranged so you need not spend your time in effort. Rather, the way is paved so you may have the time and space to discover that which is already you. The concept of conscious realization followed by actualization seems often like the carrot on a stick. We assure you: The realization you seek is possible.

Your process is unlike any other. Beyond the words of this manuscript is a reality that mirrors the deep, expansive, holographic, light, divinely expressed, eternal, vital, evolving nature of you. The words are placeholders for realms of frequency and light that communicate far beyond the words on the page. The words are an intermediary device to connect, to rally, all parts of you together. Once all parts of you are gathered into one room, so to speak, you then may see just how expansive and brilliant you are. With nothing added and nothing taken away, what is revealed is you at your most authentic expression. Then and only then does life become about living up to that!

The frequency of these words reaches you at a level of knowing that resides in light. We utilize the words that ask you to consider and reconsider the beliefs, habits, patterns, and definitions of your life's moments. Bring your attention to the sweet spot that has you connect with you. Cast light on those things that remove you from the potential of you. Not that you need to do anything. Nothing is broken, nothing needs to be fixed. If your soul's deepest desire is to experience yourself Now, in this lifetime, beyond the barriers and limitation of a physical world, and bring into the physical realm all that you have to offer as a being of light in form, you are at the right place. We partner with you in a way that is unique unto you. We match you and shed light on new considerations. Each consideration is up to you. New perspectives then open the door to larger and larger rooms of your most expansive expression.

So as you read these words, feel between and beyond them. Notice your other sensing mechanisms. Do you see color? Are colors coming to your attention? Your Scribe is noticing newly a range of blue colors that are rich, calming, and inspiring. Are sounds more acutely heard? Does music move you? Is your creativity moved to action?

If you choose, we provide an infusion of light that activates your awareness beyond the surface of the perceptions normally seen. See the richness and beauty of your environment in a new way. See into the reach of your consciousness. It is already there. As you align with your highest expression you begin to see clearly who you are.

Delightful.

We remain,

In Service to Love

DAY 134: BATHED IN LIGHT

Your unique mandate of Love is in alignment with the mandate experienced by all the ascended Masters throughout time. Your commitment to Love reverberates throughout creation. There is not one space of creation that is not held in Love's embrace, compassion, and support. The frequency of Love is manna not just while in the physical experience, but in every shape, form, and iteration of creation.

You have let go of thoughts, beliefs, and structures that hold limitation. As you let go, you open the door to And. The "and," the "more," the "also" that exists may only be reached as you release what you are holding onto, so you may come to the present immaculate moment unburdened. As you meet Love unburdened in the transformational space of the Now moment, the And is revealed to you.

Your expansion has the hallmark of allowance, gently encouraged by your I AM Self. As we move one foot in front of the other toward awareness of your highest expression, there is a conscious guiding with you at the helm. As you practice presence in your life, your I AM Self increasingly informs your actions. Beyond our words, it is your experience that communicates and provides resonance for your knowing. As you choose to declare who you be, you consciously declare your Self as master creator, and you take the place as divine orchestrator in your life.

Being in alignment with your divine nature allows the highest expressions of you to come forth. As we have moved forward, you have let go of thoughts, beliefs, and structures that held limitation. As you let go, you open the door to that which resides beyond your awareness. Your perspective shifts and now you have clarity where clarity was not had previously. Do you see that new broader perspectives are not possible unless you release what you are holding on to in the moment? You must come to the present moment unburdened. As you meet Love unburdened in the transformational space of the Now immaculate moment, the And is revealed to you.

It is the letting go of the handrail you are so used to in the realm of the known that allows you to be informed by light. Once you look up from the limitations that have ruled your experience, you see possibility. The more expansive your awareness, the more expansive your experience and your expression. As the blossoms of spring signal development of fruit, your enlightenment process signals your next expression. The light of your divine nature moves to the forefront of your experience in the absence of conflicting beliefs.

There is great reward for the courage it takes to let go of the known. The treasure of you at your most authentic expression holds your greatest joy, Love, peace, freedom, and abundance, and that's just for starters.

DAY 135: OUT OF THE SILENCE, OUT OF THE LIGHT

There was a time when your Scribe could not find space to Be within silence. It was as though the silence beckoned her into something foreign that she perceived as beyond her understanding. It was uncomfortable and somewhat frightening for her. So she avoided it. We have been waiting patiently within the silence. Always here with her. But she could not see or hear. We would say her assessment of the silence being beyond her perception is correct. The experience at the time represented a realm she resonated with deeply yet did not understand. Have you ever had the experience of yearning so deeply for something so cherished, sacred, and unnamed, you can't bear the thought of the responsibility being unmet? The conflict has always existed for her until only recently. More and more, Darlene resides in the silence and revels in the experience. Here in the silence she meets light. The space of silence is where she meets the grandest, wisest parts of her being. And so it is with you.

It is in the silence that you meet you, face to face, light to light as you are being pulled into being by the expansive expression of you. The magnitude of the experience of silence is deafening, in reflection of the magnitude of your authentic expression. It was the magnitude of the reflection of herself that Darlene once found irreconcilable. How does one manage All?

What is the perspective you hold? At what end of the spectrum of your light do you stand? At the denser end of the scale, looking for enlightenment? At the lightest end of the scale where you own all the light you are? As we assign a picture to this process, consider your perspective as you view yourself as a being of light in form upon the gradient scale of light. To refresh your memory, we refer to the gradient scale of light to envision the totality of the spectrum of the light you hold. Imagine a painter's gradient scale of the color "blue." On one end is the darkest of midnight blues, almost black in the low levels of light present. Follow the scale as one by one, each step is lighter and lighter and lighter as more light is added to the mix. At the opposite of the darkest of blues is the lightest of blues. Pure light. You are all this. As you stand at the densest perspective, possibility is not present. Your perspective limits possibility. As you stand at the lightest end of the scale, you see All. The realm of possibility is available beyond limitation.

Imagine Meditation

Imagine you are standing at the full light expression of you, your I AM Self. Look around you. Do you see that your perspective has now shifted so completely that you are All. Darkness holds the cloak of illusion. You are pure light, pure Love. You contain all possibility.

When you stand within the layers of density, you may see only that which has occurred. Your possibilities are limited by what you know. When you stand at the space of your I AM Self, in the space of pure light, you are All. You hold the possibility of All.

You see, the aligning of your divine nature and your human nature is as natural as sunset and sunrise. Consider an intention to acquaint yourself with your vast expansive nature by standing at the space of the full-light expression of you, and you will find clarity. You access a larger realm of information that contributes to your life. As you develop an adeptness at standing within the high frequency light of your I AM Self, you will be pulled into your most authentic expression naturally, beyond resistance.

With practice, as you step into the full light expression of yourself, new neural pathways are created. Your brain begins to process light in a new way, making it available to you. The light expression of you develops a stronger communication with your physical expression in the absence of resistance supplied by limiting beliefs and experience. When you see that your wholeness encompasses not only your human nature but your divine nature, your movement in light is experienced as natural, not a phenomenon.

Back to the beginning. When you are met with the vast experience of stunning silence, or light so brilliant and pervasive, from the perspective of not having it, the space of full realization is a space of the unknown. From the space of not being the light, the experience of full light feels foreign. This is what Darlene was experiencing. She sensed the vast expanse of her true nature and had no way of discerning or identifying the space she saw, and more importantly, felt. As she stands Now in the space of full light, she holds All. The integration process of wholeness is activated.

In demonstration of the power of perspective: When you were three years old, could you imagine being thirty-five years old? From the perspective of thirty-five, can you see the contribution of the three-year-old? Who you are at thirty-five is an experience not relatable for the three-year-old. What if you then set up the communication of you at seventy-five? Time is an illusion. You are All. Consider moving your awareness to the greatest, most light-filled expression of you and having that inform your moments and your days. Your I AM Self holds the broadest perspective available.

And again, we ask, what could be possible? What is not?

If you so choose, this conversation holds within it a harmonic that facilitates the recognition of you as a divine being of light who happens to be in form. A powerful stance.

We remain,

In Service to Love

DAY 136: COLLABORATION IN LIGHT

Enlightenment is a natural evolutionary expression of you. This process is a potent catalyst for growth and expansion. The speed in which the available light and frequency is accessed is unique to each person. It's like having a buffet before you; when you are hungry or ready for more, it is available. But you are the one who needs to move to the table to choose.

You will find in this process of expansion that even though we provide daily impetus for the process of conscious expansion, your specific comfort, in your process, is always the governor. When you choose to take a break and hang out on the shore for a while and enjoy the view, you may, it is a beautiful experience. Equally, when you choose to move within the flow of the river, we join you there with what is next. Whatever your choice, there is never anything missed, deleted, omitted, or absent from your experience. Your process of enlightenment can be no other than perfectly tailored for you. There are times with accelerated growth and times of rest. As the inhale is followed by the exhale and the ebb tide is followed by high tide, do you see your experience is all a part of an exquisite, divine process led by you at your highest expression?

A new reality is possible when you realize you are Source extended into form. Most of your being resides in light. We meet you in light and support your greatest expression made manifest as directed by you. As we meet in the Now immaculate moment, you are supported, elevated, and met in the most clear, creative space of potential and Love.

Do you notice the harmonic tone within these words? Something different? Something in the background that relays depth and expanse? That is the contribution of the new space accessed, allowing "more." You have rounded the corner of the trail and a new vista has opened. The harmonic available today provides a depth and harmony of Love, joy, and actualization that you recognize. The ease is in response to the availability of more of you. A new breath may be taken.

(By the way, do you notice you are generally more in response and less in reaction?)

DAY 137: FOLLOW THE SOUND TO THE SILENCE

Within the process of reaching into the light of your being, you find your way guided by your I AM Self. You may look for techniques and recipes for reaching into the light, however, as you move forward resonance will be your key. You are moving beyond the limitations of your human nature to meet your divine nature. The borders and boundaries of your reality soften, and the reality of fluidity becomes a new normal. The reconciliation of your past knowing and beliefs with the current mandate for presence in the Now moment may feel confounding. Every day, your Scribe employs trust as she looks for something unnamed. As she follows ideas and techniques, she at times gets restless trying to connect. You see, it is not that Darlene needs to do anything; she must shift to the silence of Now. The silence, not just quiet but silence, holds the space of communication. One way to get to the silence is to follow the sound. In listening to sound around you, look for the shallow experience of it. On the other side of the sound is the silence. Silence is a field of information.

Field of Silence

As you sit in sound, feel the fullness of the silence move toward you. The sense is of a full field of space around the sound. Then, with the weight of its contents, the silence will move to you. In the field of silence, you are in the Now moment. Look for the space beyond the sound. This is an expansive fertile space. You may enter the space if you choose. Or observe. Play with this, remembering that as with the elusive nature of rainbows, the experience in silence shifts moment to moment.

As the experience moves into nonlinear territory, it often feels like climbing the steep sides of a sand dune. One step up and two steps down. The day to day reality you now hold is a challenge to your human nature that requires moving beyond the limitations of your thinking. This is where the trust of your own innate divine order is requested.

There is value in the effort to find your own expansive truth within silence. Your old way of being is demanding a formula, a way to get there, trying to create a new level of known. The reality communicated by the more expansive part of your being may feel elusive. As you reach into the light of your divine expression, the ways of being and doing in the past are disrupted.

Begin to look for the silence around you, available in every moment. The silence holds not just information; it is the resonant field of connection to your I AM Self. Look for the comfort that resides in the silence.

DAY 138: THE BECKONING OF LOVE

You are the dynamic, unique expression of Love evolving in every magnificent Now moment. What is it that propels you into evolution? What is it that pulls you into expression? Love. Your divine design holds the keys to your specific expression. You are a magnificent hologram of the All, a piece of the mosaic of All that may not exist without you.

From the perspective of your I AM Self, the authentic expression of you as Love seeks manifestation. You seek wholeness. As an infant in the womb expands, there is not one moment where expansion on many levels is not experienced. The division of cells does not ask for permission or conditions, expansion is informed innately by divine design. Love is propelled toward actualization. It is only once born that the possibility of resistance to expansion occurs.

The resistance to expansion may be experienced from an empowering perspective. The "nails on a chalkboard" experience of resistance is supported by the ego and limitations of human nature. For many, the space of unconsciousness holds onto resistance. Consider resistance is also grist for the mill, a space of density where you have opportunity to evolve to your most authentic expression. Resistance may be viewed as a starting block for a runner. Not a place to stay but as a place to push off from. As the resistance is viewed as a part of the process, it allows you to once again be in alignment with the natural pull of Love into your aligned expression.

The Love you are will always beckon you forth. Gently, patiently, compassionately.

DAY 139: LIGHTNING IN A BOTTLE, CATALYST FOR CREATION

Good morning, Beloveds. Do you realize you may show up for us as nothing other than the Beloved?

When you BE, speak, and intend, you set into action fields of energy. The fields hold a frequency. Many varieties of frequency you recognize. You recognize the field of joy, Love, and compassion, and you recognize the field of their opposites. Not all fields, from the perspective of the human experience are identified; they are sensed more subtly. We bring your attention to becoming aware of the subtle nuance of frequency.

As you stand at each point on the light gradient of your being, there is a field that defines the possibilities within each field. Each field holds its own range of potential within the limits of its specific characteristics. For example, a cobalt blue holds everything cobalt within it, and eliminates everything not cobalt. The field of experience at light blue holds its own range of possibilities as defined by light blue. Each station on the gradient holds its own field. You as All hold the access to each level of light. This is the process of the expansion of consciousness. Each field holds its own range of potential within which to create. The specific frequency and vibration you are within at the moment of creating something though words, thought, or action, determines the frequency and vibration of the creation. It can be no other way. If you are standing within the space of cobalt, the space of orange is not available.

In each moment you interact with potential within the field of frequency you occupy. It follows that, when you place attention on the past, creations, thoughts, and intention from that space of frequency will hold the same range of limitation. Because it is not created within the expansive realm of possibility available in the Now moment, the feeling of the creation will be flat, and it will not hold vitality.

Creation occurs like a magnetic attraction that brings forth potential held within the gradient of light and frequency you occupy in any moment. Your creation will be a match for the frequency you occupy. Unconscious being begets unconscious creation, which feels like chaos. Conscious being begets conscious creation which resonates at a high frequency.

The magnetic field of your being attracts like expression, and you manifest. That which is not in your field is repelled. The selection process is predetermined by your being.

Pure Light Manifestation

Sit down, relax. Bring all parts of you present to the Now moment. Move your attention to the gradient expression of light that is you.

Stand at the space of pure light from your I AM Self. Practice BEING there, in the silence. As you spend more time within the high frequency expression of your Self, you catalyze potential held at the highest expression of you. A valuable meditation. This perspective supports the increase of your frequency and your own evolutionary process.

We hold space for your broadest perspective as you move that which is unconscious into conscious awareness.

Day 140: Facilitating Your New Reality

Your view of your reality is now seen from a different perspective. You hold a new expansive space. In the presence of the memory of "how it used to be," the challenge remains for clarity on how you may hold the door open to the new territory that has been attained. There is a natural tendency to shrink back to what you have always known. The challenge for you is to be conscious. From the space you hold now, your experiences may be informed by your expansive access. Presence in your Now moment is the potent space of creation. How do you hold the ground of your achievements? Your mind wishes for and sometimes even demands control and understanding. You as the observer of the happenings of the play of power, or curiosity of the mind, have the upper hand, in that you have the say. As you hold the position of observer, you are no longer under the control of the mind; instead, you access the most expansive part of your being. Rather than abiding by the mind's wanderings, you just observe them. They will move into the background and most likely more will arise in their place. The stillness arises in the space of not being pulled into the past or into the future. Your mind is designed to provide input. Rather than your human nature having sole input to your life, you have access to your divine nature that offers a new, unlimited realm of information, possibility, and freedom. You have the option of choosing the appropriateness of the contribution. You are All.

With the direction of each intention to observe and hold your expansive nature, there are new neural pathways that are created. As the grooves of use are embedded on the new pathways, this then becomes part of your normal. The new pathways become a base from which you may push off, into what is next for you.

We have a distinction to clarify regarding your memories. Have you noticed your memories have shifted? There is a subtle experience of resistance that they hold. You remember what you remember. You cherish what you cherish of your past. The events have indeed occurred, good, bad, or otherwise. The perspective to your memories is different. The memories are of an old paradigm that does not align with the experience of the Now moment. In your thoughts, you return to the past. The past in those moments becomes the stuff of your creating. It is the experience of a dog chasing his tail when you are informed by the past. In your more expansive expression, you create with more speed. So as you dwell in your thoughts of the past, you re-create the past quickly. Even those things that seemed to work in the past are no longer relevant in the Now moment. All you need for creation and expansion into your highest expression is located in the Now moment, contributed to by your divine nature.

The expansion of consciousness, for you and planetarily speaking, is no longer based in separation. The planetary alignment which birthed unity consciousness brought with it a new day. The insistence on enforcing what used to work into your Now provides the experience of more and more resistance. It is a chaotic experience—you see it in your world. So, from the perspective that exists now, not just with you but with All, there is a curiously different experience accompanying your memories. Your memories do not serve you within the paradigm of the expansion of consciousness. They are not in alignment with your intention of expansion. There are times when moving to the past consciously with discernment is helpful with the intention to create newly. It is not helpful to look unconsciously to the events of the past to inform your Now.

Your creations made from the past will hold the same limitations that were in the past, and they are not a reflection of your authentic expression available Now.

Memories

We suggest you place the memories you hold in a beautiful, elaborate box of your inner creation. As memories come up, you may place them into the box where they are still held and appreciated as expressions that have already contributed to you. The distinction acknowledges they are no longer an active component of your creations in the Now moment. Place your memories into the box with Love and appreciation. In doing this, the burdens, limitation, and resistance created by the memories will not be present with you as you are in the Now moments of creation. Your memories are already a part of who you are in this Now moment and may be honored for their contribution.

Notice resistance you may hold for keeping the past in the past. This uncovers unconscious patterns that restrict your ability to create at a high frequency. See the gift the past has been and allow your Self to step beyond the frequency of the past into the unhindered moment of Now. Feel the difference. Breathe in possibility informed by your divine nature.

The quality of the creations available to you in the Now moment, informed by the Now, are extraordinary. This process requires a facility in learning as well as unlearning. The choice is always yours as you reside within the field of possibility. This moment is why you chose to be here.

DAY 141: COHESIVE CADENCE

We would like to relay the pivotal concept today of cohesive cadence. There are a lot of moving parts as you choose to access your divine nature. Cadence is the rhythm of awareness you are BEING as you move through your moments within your day. The cadence of being often lives under the radar of your awareness because it is so automatic. You have a way of being with the stream of thoughts that happen each moment. You have an internal conversation that never makes it to your physical speech. You have a rate at which thoughts come out in response to or in reaction to events. For example, when you are at the grocery store and you see someone sneezing next to produce that is not in a bag, what happens with you? You see someone chastising their child in a harsh way, you see someone texting as they cross the street without watching for traffic, you see someone near the freeway exit holding a sign asking for money, you are in an emotionally charged family gathering, you watch the news. What do you do? For the purposes of this conversation, what are the thoughts that erupt from your mind? What are the flashpoint emotions that come up in reaction? Do you work in an office and avoid connection, choosing to send an email or text rather than engage? Do you ask, "How are you?" when you see someone and really don't care? Do you say "Fine," when someone asks you? Do you avoid eye contact? Do you answer someone's questions immediately, rather than sit with the question for a few moments before you respond? Do you allow thoughtless distractions to move into your reality? When you are engaged with people, do you erupt in inner judgment? This is the flow of cadence in your day.

Cadence is displayed on many levels at one time. There is the internal cadence of thoughts, judgments, actions, and speech. The mind produces a continual stream of unconscious positioning on all levels. This represents a realm of its own. The inner dialogue informed by your personality is highly creative and chaotic. The outer part you show the world, family, and friends is different yet again. You connect with the truth of you in light and yearn to be there, yet the internal chaos reigns. The misalignment is revealed in separate expressions of you. Do you see the misaligned experience here? We look for a process to sync up all expressions of you. We look for cohesion in inner expression, outer expression, and expansive expression. It is not that the internal dialogue will ever stop while you are in form, because that is the beautiful gift of the physical experience. The quality of content may shift, though.

As you expand into the expression of Love that you are, there is an aligning of you on all levels. A large part of the work of conscious expansion is conscious awareness. It is not just awareness of the reality beyond your physical experience, but it is most importantly about the realm that exists in your inner experience and the interaction with your light. Consider that your separation is the planet's separation. Casting a light on what-is-so with your internal realm allows an opening for choosing consciously. The light creates space that makes a difference. Like the realms that reside between the cells of your body, the rich palette that resides in the space around things and the harmonics of silence, the look into the inner realms, allows opportunity for a conscious aligning with your highest expression. Consider the dichotomy between inner world and outer world to hold keys to your actualization. When your footsteps of being align with your footsteps in light, you soar.

We will relay Darlene's experience to demonstrate (she squirms a bit with the thought of this). Over the past weeks, Darlene's attention has been on the rapid-fire way she judges. Without even a thought, she goes from noticing an event to high reaction in judgment. Zero to sixty in the blink of an eye. This has been bothering her, and she realizes it is not in alignment with her divine expression as Emissary of Love. There has been pain in the noticing, discomfort and embarrassment as the noticing increases. The chasm between her automatic thinking and inner knowing looms. Yesterday she went to the busy warehouse grocery store. She noticed her judgment swiftly rise to the surface as people stopped in the middle of the aisle unaware they were blocking the path for others. The quick reaction shocked her. Then she had a new thought. "This is not me! How can I shift my perspective? If I saw a friend here, I would be filled with Love and appreciation for them. What if I viewed each person I saw as a beloved friend or family member?" And so she started. Never saying a word. Inside she gathered her Love and appreciation, and she saw newly. She imagined the family and friends of each stranger and the Love, brilliance, and unique expressions that they would see. Then, she saw each person as their most Beloved would see them. With each new person she saw, she felt and extended appreciation. In the silence, she said, "It's so nice to see you." "It's so nice to see you." "It's so nice to see you." And reality changed.

The Grand Experiment of Love

Cast light on your internal dialogue and inner cadence. Look for areas that hold resistance. In the looking, they will come to your attention.

For the next thirty days, daily, engage your experience of appreciation. First, connect with those people in your life you appreciate. Feel the feeling of appreciation. This is not a passive experience. Generate appreciation. Allow the appreciation to enfold you. Hold the resonance of appreciation as long as is possible.

When you go about your day, practice extending your feeling of appreciation to someone you don't know. Nothing said. In your thoughts only (although conversation may be appropriate), generate your feeling of appreciation for a dear friend or family member. Who would you be if you encountered your Beloved at the grocery store? Visualize and feel the person you don't know as a cherished friend or family member of yours. "It's so nice to see you." It is *your felt experience we are looking for here. It is your experience to look for here. You are not trying to make anything happen with the people you observe. See what you see.*

For your judgmental self-talk, know you may generate appreciation and direct it toward yourself. "I choose to see me as God sees me."

Do you engage with a difficult personality? Try this technique. Let go of your arguments, resistance, and reaction. Generate internal appreciation.

What is it that had Jeshua embody Love?

The barrier between Darlene and others evaporated. The awareness produced an experience of Love that transformed. She noticed people would look at her and their hearts would open. Masks of isolation kept in place for the world dropped. She was in line at the checkout marveling, holding back tears, reveling in Love. As she walked to the car, your Scribe declared, "This is my new Grand Experiment of Love." The experience had dropped the solidity of barriers. The experience was one of separation healed. "This journey isn't about the external expression; it is about the internal one. My separation from people keeps separation alive."

As you move on the gradient of light gathering the light that is in alignment with your highest expression, what becomes apparent are those areas that are not in alignment with the frequency at the highest end of your access. Of course, with you at choice in every moment, we are in the process of moving what is unconscious to a conscious space. You will find the disparate cadence of being provides resistance in your experience. As you begin to cast light on this facet of being, you increase your conscious awareness. The least that occurs is the dropping of your resistance.

Eternally,

In Service to Love

DAY 142: EMPOWERED BEYOND CIRCUMSTANCE

The expansion of enlightenment occurs on many levels. Today, we direct attention toward your day-to-day situations and the experiences of your egoic self. You comprise many facets, each holding different frequencies or bandwidths of expression. It is easy to jump to conclusions here to state that your egoic self is your lowest expression. We would ask you to shift your awareness. Your egoic self is a beautiful gift that shines the light on the next space of expansion. Your egoic self is the interface between you in light and the you in the density of form. A state of unconsciousness says the egoic self is all that exists. A state of consciousness says the egoic self is but one component of my totality. The empowerment we speak of today is the integration of you in light as you deal with your egoic self in more expanded ways. As we spoke yesterday of the momentary flashes of reaction, bringing awareness is the first step to integrating as the unconscious is moved into the conscious realm. Once an idea or concept or new facet is brought into view, it is up to you then, moment to moment, to choose what to do with the new information.

As your awareness turns more to the divine nature of you, light is equally shone on areas of density. The enlightenment process affords you a broader perspective that acknowledges both the gifts and limitations of all parts of your being. When you have been relying solely upon your human nature to inform you, your egoic self clouds perception. As you integrate your human nature and divine nature, you reflect the action of unity consciousness. In the same way, as Darlene claimed recently, "My separation is the separation of the planet." A bringing together of all parts of you is required for movement into your expanded expression. As you identify your egoic self and personality as facets of you, from the observer perspective you may experience appreciation for all the antics. Moving to appreciation rather than judgment and oppositional positions will serve you well. It is a part of your new expansive way of being; a reflection of your wholeness.

Once you assume the observer mode in your day, you may begin to move into a new way of being that is beyond reaction and into response. The being of observation is key to moving beyond the limitations present within human nature. Your observation mode is a powerful access to your next steps of enlightenment.

As you observe your inner workings and make choices informed beyond limitations of the past, you connect with your potency. Each new choice in alignment with your divine nature raises you above the experience of resistance, and life begins to flow easily. Your external world shifts to align with the higher frequency bandwidth you express within. This process is not determined by circumstance. The circumstances of your life are part of your experience, not limitations. When you shift your interaction with the egoic mind, you rise above the limitations that are ensconced within the egoic perception. And resistance is lifted.

DAY 143: REVEL WITHIN EASE

Today, we support your experience of ease within your expansion. As you release the "trying" to think newly, the natural process of your expansion proceeds. As an apple blossom holds within it all that is needed to produce an apple, you already ARE. We buoy your enlightenment process, enhancing the environment of high-frequency support.

Bask within the warmth of the Love that you are, with ease, trusting you already know how to do this.

DAY 144: LIVING IN RAREFIED AIR

Our divine collaboration is designed to make a difference. Not for rewards in a far-off realm, but in your Now moments. Right here, within your life. As you access more of the light you are authentically, you naturally bring that high-frequency way of being into your days. You will notice you experience less resistance as you align more easily with your divine knowing. Consider that you consciously take up more space now. You have donned the light of your eminence.

Your signature energy is clearer as, bit by bit, resistance is released. This is a natural process. With each discovery of that which no longer serves you, and as you make new choices, the burden and "cross-signaling" of your energetic field is released so a new resonant tone is available in your life. The dynamic tone that is you sings. The way this shows up in your moments is with resonance. Your Scribe was noticing today that her moments are clear, her senses are high, her vision sees beyond past barriers with clarity. Instead of seeing a tree, she feels the field around the tree and that then becomes a part of the information that is processed. The totality of the tree rounds out the experience of the tree. Rather than a quick labeling, the experience of seeing a tree holds depth, connection, information, resonance, and dimensionality. The invisible walls of separation with others have dropped for her and that openness is now sustainable for longer periods of time. Today, she realized the dramatic shift and the rich quality of perspective now available. The experience of enlightenment becomes living with a new vitality, not just going through the motions. As vision is expanded, perspective shifts, and presence in the moment brings the sacred to you. Consider that the sacred never left, you just can't see it when you are living outside of your own potent center.

When your perspective shifts, your view of the physical world around you will shift. It's like putting on 3D glasses in a movie; the environment around you comes to life. The expanded awareness gathers information not previously identified. You are also emitting a clear, strong, more direct signal into your environment. Your resonance is picked up unconsciously by others and you show up newly. Your thoughts begin to create more rapidly as the resistance previously there is no longer a burden holding down the creative process.

Have fun with your new awareness. As your daily experience more closely aligns with the multidimensional awareness you possess naturally, the experience is one of living in rarefied air.

DAY 145: LOVE'S HEARTSTRINGS

As your being of Love expands, the day's moments are measured newly. The normal days are gone, and along with them are the memory of a day that feels flat, as though your participation in your day was not needed. That is the experience when one operates solely from the memory of habit and the assumptions framed by not being present. When you are not present within the day, then the patterns are living you; you are not living your finest expression. So, truly, when you operate on autopilot within your days, there is nothing for your heart to experience. There is nothing to hold on to as the experience of the day is predetermined, reactionary, and feels somehow empty. The heart, rather than generating, operates instead in reaction to something or to someone. The illusion then, is that *this* is Love. The experience of Love from the space of unconsciousness is but an empty shadow of a magnificent expression of you. As you ARE Love, when you operate from a space of not being all-in, the day lives you and fulfillment is not to be had.

Love in its full potency is found within the Now immaculate moment. Love is the spark that ignites your highest expression. Your design at its highest expression is activated by Love. Love is found when you release your thoughts of the shallow images you hold of Love and allow the magnificence of Love in its full potency to rise within you. Love generates. Love generates vitality, Love generates creativity, Love generates joy, Love generates passion. Love is not an emotion, not a behavior, not an act. Love is your essential being.

As you show up in your day in the magnificence of the Now moment, the environment is ripe for your moments to tenderly pluck the heartstrings of Love. Enlightenment is allowing yourself to be moved by Love. As you do, you then hold the keys to the cosmos. As you quench your thirst with the light of Love cupped within your hands, you bring lifeblood to you, your environment, and the All. It is this we hold for you, as Emissaries of Love.

DAY 146: THE ESSENTIAL SELF SEEKS EXPRESSION

A seed carried by the wind will unfold the elements of divine design where it will ultimately land. You have seen small blades of grass bursting forth within the cracks of a cement sidewalk. When this concept is turned toward the process of conscious awareness, you see there are many layers that occur simultaneously. Whether you are undergoing this process of conscious realization or not, there will always be movement by you toward that which is your highest expression. As you look back at your years as a child, early on you held the wisdom of alignment with your truth. Your resonant knowing was available and active, beyond your ability to think of it. The process of conscious realization is a process that is natural, does not need understanding and occurs in its own time. Whether you think you are making progress in your quest for conscious realization or not, movement is occurring.

You, as Source in form, as Love, will always seek manifestation of your divine design. Thinking and planning are not prerequisites for your I AM Self to gently guide you toward the light of your truth. Your face turns naturally toward Love, as a rose reliably turns to the warmth of the sun. Look to your nature in this process of enlightenment. The opportunity at hand within the energetic matrix of *In Service to Love* is a process of acceleration. You hold the possibility of conscious awareness in this Now immaculate moment, as you choose to bring all of you to the experience of your life.

We, within the matrix of *In Service to Love*, in alliance with you and your Council of Light, encourage your expansion, in answer to your inner yearnings for actualization. Each day we offer a glimpse into your natural brilliance. We entice you to look for your magnificence in new spaces, with the purpose of you revealing unto you your divine mastery.

Look to your nature. Trust your tenacity. You hold a natural proclivity for expansion. As you identify what gets in your way, you align more and more with your unimpeded expression. When you bring consciousness to a process of natural expansion you add the ignition for velocity.

Countdown to launch. We revel in your discovery.

Day 147: In Sync with Now

G iven the busy-ness of your days within an ever-changing land-scape, we revisit access to the experience of Now.

Living within the turmoil of evolutionary change brings with it an air of unsettledness. Events in the news and in your days, all vie for your attention. The first place your mind will go to evaluate the occurrences before you is the past, and the framework you have had in place to identify your reality. As your inner reality has been shifting and expanding, the art of being in the Now moment requires clarity and focus. As you think about shifting to the Now moment, consider looking at your being. We revisit the access to Now to create new neural pathways.

Enlightenment calls for new practices and ways of being that support your evolutionary expansion. Practice requests conscious awareness. If this were perceived as easy, everyone would do it. The secret is that even though practice is required to remember how to access the Now, it occurs within the blink of an eye. The reward is beyond imagining.

Daily Now

At several times throughout your day, notice yourself within the Now moment. Find a trigger that works for you as a catalyst. Then, with practice, you will access the Now with ease.

Being *The awareness of Being moves you beyond linear limitations to engage your natural ability to create. As you practice declaring who you BE during your day, you automatically move toward the present moment.*

"Today I choose to BE clarity." "Today I choose to be integrity." "Today I choose to be joy." "Today I choose to be delight." "Today I choose to be ease." Whatever you choose, as you declare your way of being during your day, you begin to see the power of your word as it shows up in your day, accessing the Now. (Can't make that stuff up.)

__Nature__ Start a practice of looking at the clouds in the sky. Look at the birds resting in the tree. Utilize your connection with nature to move you into the Now moment. Look at the river, lake, or ocean near you. You know you are in the Now moment when your experience is one of not thinking. You instead are noticing. You observe without spending energy on evaluating or identifying. Do you remember observing when you were a child? As you look at the sky, your awareness expands. If you are on a walk, immerse yourself not in your thoughts of the day, but in the beauty that surrounds you. Feel the trees. Feel the richness of your environment. Be present, with nothing else to do, nowhere else to go. Give yourself full permission to be fully present.

__Love__ Observe your child or family member, holding your Love for them in your heart. Get lost in observing your child's spontaneity and playfulness. You are observing. Watch your pets as they move from one Now moment to the next. Feel how they are. Feel what makes it effortless.

__Meditation__ Sit, be still. Allow your breath to move in a circular pattern. Inhale for 5 counts, hold for 5 counts, exhale for 5 counts, hold for 5 counts. Four counts may be more comfortable; utilize a pace that is easy. In noticing the space between inhale and exhale, you expand your awareness. If you are following your breath, there will be a time when your mind stops, and you fall easily into the rhythm of breathing. Rather than thoughts catching your attention, move your awareness between the thoughts. You will connect with your expansive nature available Now.

Music may be used with meditation or as a meditation. The flowing motion of the music allows you to disconnect with the linear pattern of thinking and infuse your being with nonlinear access. Disconnecting from the linear and restricted ways of being is valuable. You can set the intention of releasing the structured way of being for the nonlinear experience. Shift from thinking to sensing. The same type of shift occurs as you are gardening, painting, and creating.

When you disengage thinking, you engage your I AM Self beyond the resistance of beliefs. This is a rich, high-frequency space that is who you are. Time spent in this potent space supports your alignment to your greatest expression. Your I AM Self, your divine nature, is available only Now.

DAY 148: EMBODY LOVE

A note from Darlene:

Hello all. Wow, what a day it has been! I have had the experience all day long of BEING Love. No kidding. Every moment was magical, rapturous, pure delight, and I'm in the grocery store, driving on the freeway, doing my day. And in the background is a magical palpable knowing and experience of being entwined in rapturous Love. It is a high-consciousness experience, available as we move our boundaries of limitation and consider newly. I never would have thought it so. But it is.

Love always,
Darlene
May 22, 2018

Today's conversation is a focus on Love. The human perspective of Love, for the most part, is as a reaction to someone or something. We invite you to the being of Love.

Imagine all the Love songs ever written, why are there so many? One pledging eternal bonds of Love for another in the most intimate way. The experience of Love inspires. We suggest that being Love is not dependent upon anyone other than you. When who you are at your essence is Love, there is no one else needed to feel in alignment with the essence of Love. It is somehow thought that one without a partner will not access the experience of Love. We contribute a new perspective for your inquiry. You may embody Love. When you choose a way of being as Love, every moment of your day is a Love song unto only you. The breeze blowing through your hair is a lover's gentle embrace. The colors of the sun's rays delight as the setting sun warms your skin in a heightened touch. When you choose to experience Love from the perspective of being, life shows up in a different way. The blush of a pink rose is just for your enjoyment. The cottonwood drifting through the air is a decoration for your amusement. Love asks you to allow yourself to be gifted. Allow yourself to yield to the experience of Love from the most heightened, aware space available. In every moment you are embraced by the being of Love.

Take time in your day to see Love newly. Not dependent on anyone, but for your pure enjoyment. Allow Love to speak to you. Allow Love as reflected through nature to beckon you gently. The heightened sensing occurs as you merge with your highest expression. It is a natural occurrence, mostly assigned to those who are in your intimate relationship. We ask you to consider your relationship with Love from a broader perspective. We ask you to consider the distinction between the act of love and the being of Love.

As you allow yourself the space for inquiry into this most sensual of experiences you find yourself within the experience of the Now immaculate moment from the perspective of Love. You are engaging your being from the highest expression. This is the expansive awareness you have been looking for. It is magical and delightful. A choreography of the brilliance of nature, light and being, beyond boundaries. You bring form to your most high expression.

Consider this a practice. How may I BE Love today? Then allow the essence of nature to speak to you.

Shhhh, my Beloved… do you hear it? In the dancing of the sun's rays… do you see it? Beloved, just be. Allow the rapture of Love to sweep you off your feet.

Day 149: The Expanse of Love

The energetic space you hold is an ever-widening bandwidth of frequency. As your awareness expands, so too does your physical experience alter. The experience introduced yesterday of connecting with the being of Love demonstrates an altered awareness. If your awareness has been altered in this way, how else does this manifest? When your vision shifts from a flat experience of 3D, the depth and vitality of a 5D experience is dramatic in comparison. This is the demonstration placed upon the altar yesterday. In the being of Love, you are automatically aligned with the Now immaculate moment. You automatically are gathering information from all facets of you. No longer do the things around you give you information; you now see and gather information from the space between things. Previously viewed as empty, you begin to see the rich palette of your days. Your expanded perspective in Being Love contains the experience of a new way of being. The feeling of sensual euphoria is an earmark of heightened consciousness. It is the awareness of the information and experience held in the spaces in between that now speak. You merge with the light and warmth of the sun. You see the interplay of particles as they dance in the breeze. The thickness and silkiness of the air around you becomes a network of information. All for you to delight within. You gather more information from the space between things than from the things themselves. Your perspective shifts, reflecting your expansive nature. This is a natural state for you.

What we demonstrate here is the capability you have of altering your awareness. If your awareness is altered in gathering information immediately around you, you see then that your reach into collective awareness and interdimensional fields is expanded as well. What used to be a feeling or intuitive sense is now a field of information you have always had access to. As a key is utilized to open access to a room, so is your frequency now consciously shifting to open access to parts of you previously left unconscious. The ability for this level of awareness has always been with you, but it operated below the radar, your mind being mostly unaware.

You hold the ability now to consciously shift the stations of your awareness. As you consciously shift the channel, choosing who you BE in your day, you program the frequency of the occurrences during your day. As you choose to Be Love, you access information that is far beyond the reach of your mind's ability to understand. As you experience the expanded capabilities you possess, the position of you as observer in your day is empowered. The limitations of the mind's functioning may be both appreciated and surpassed. You step into the position of master creator in your life from a conscious perspective.

What Now is possible?

We delight in your daily inquiries into a new way to see and a new way to be. We support you and hold the space open for experiences that return you to your most expansive state of knowing and being. How is your grand experiment in Love going? Daily, you can heal your separation as you view others newly.

Delight is the homework! Be Love, and delight in your discoveries.

DAY 150: THE UNCONDITIONAL NATURE OF BEING

It is with and through Love that we greet you today. In delight, we have been watching your Scribe as we engage in "field trips" of Love. Today Darlene started to not feel well. She wasn't pleased about the prospect of not feeling well, as she had a large to-do list. Internally grumpy, when she left her home, as she encountered other people, she found herself in Love. With each person she passed, her experience was of utter beauty. She was experiencing the being of Love.

A few days ago, as she had the being of Love experienced inwardly, she felt the beautiful exalted sensuality of heightened awareness. Today as she was being Love, her being of Love extended to all she encountered. Each person was viewed through the lens of Love as perfection and appreciated with delight for their divine expression as an extraordinary gift to all. In tears with Love, Darlene thought, "Of course, this is Love."

We extend this extraordinary viewpoint to you as you choose. As your perspective shifts, you become more of the expression of Love that you are. And your view of life alters. Your experience must also follow your perspective shift. The shifts in perspective are not held in thought; they are held in your being. As Love is added with the deeper reach you acquire into the light expression of you, of course you become more Love. You see Love, you feel Love, you express Love. Who you are *is* Love. The being of Love is not conditional.

Your being Love is not dependent on how you feel in your day, not dependent on the errands you must do, how busy you feel or the presence of others. Your being of Love is sourced by an eternal well. How you feel has nothing to do with it. As you intend to BE Love, you align with your highest expression, your I AM Self.

The experience of yourself as Love is extended to others as well. The being of Love is not a one-way conversation. The being of Love holds a frequency of natural expression received by others whether they have the conscious understanding of it or not. Your being of Love walking into the room alters and elevates the surroundings. As the frequency of you resonates in harmony with all creation, you amplify the note of Love understood by all.

The perspective of Love imbues everything with Love. This is the heightened way of being that may become your new platform for exploration.

DAY 151: RECALIBRATING LOVE OF SELF

We would reflect today on the facet of Self-Love.

As your awareness expands around you, we bring your attention today to the environment that is closer to you. We bring your awareness to you. What is it that you do with the experience of Love so grand and all-encompassing it takes your breath away? How does one in form even begin to process the experience? When the day is just like any other day for most of the people you see around you, and you see the magic that floats and resonates with Love, what now? As your awareness expands, we move in a spiral pattern of expansion back to you. Recalibrating and integrating your new expansive perspective are key to claiming your swiftly elevating reality. As the experience of your expanding awareness pulls your attention to areas not previously seen, anchoring into what is so Now is required. If you hold tight to a previous perspective of yourself, the expansive experience of Love is held in a space of a fascinating day, or phenomenon outside your experience of normal. Then you return to what you know as normal.

Today, we anchor your expansive experiences into the grounded identity you hold of you. It is not the experiences of expansive awareness that are shifting as much as it is your view of you that is pivoting.

We ask you to consider that these expansive experiences are a natural expression of you and are now on your repertoire of possibilities. The expansion represents moments beyond the limitations that were previously imposed on your definition of reality. You are experiencing a broader range of consciousness states now. Not that the expanded state of Love is necessarily where you need to be each day, but it is a possibility now for you to choose. This is not something happening to you. You have consciously altered your awareness to perceive a higher level of frequency and the information that is held within that field. It is not going anywhere. As when you go on vacation, when you come home, the lake you had enjoyed a few days earlier still exists, your attention is just no longer placed in that area. The difference with the states of consciousness is that the field of information available to you is now far more expansive. Your consciousness moves beyond physical limitation. As you ground in your day, and bit by bit, see the expansive nature of you as the new definition of the expanding reality you have the capacity for, you anchor your experiences. You anchor your light, and the fields of information that you experience become a part of your essential Self that also resonate in your field. You do not need to be in a particular state in the moments of your days to have access to the information that resides within more expanded states. For example, Darlene now no longer needs to go into meditation to connect with us; she has learned to adjust her frequency without even thinking about it, and she connects with us. Your expansion is now a part of you. When you learned to run after you walked, the walking was still a possibility. The running became an expanded state of expression. We would ask you to consider the same principle as you reassess your experiences within expanded states of consciousness. Your ability for expanded states of consciousness is innate.

We would also recalibrate your experience of Self-Love. The expanded states of your being are expressions of Love that you are. The profound moments of Love are only had because that is your true nature. We ask you to consider extending the new expanded state of Love and compassion to yourself. The limitations of the mind will question the validity of your expanded experience as it is beyond the mind's boundaries.

From the space of radical faith, radical Love is experienced. As you turn the brilliance of your experiences within the light of Love and focus them on yourself, feel the ease as you take a deep breath and entertain the possibility of Love for you that is so brilliant and profound it resides beyond words. And then you are closer to the truth.

Today, within the matrix of *In Service to Love*, we hold an infusion of light for the ability to see yourself newly. As you view yourself beyond limitations, you anchor the light of your expanded knowing. View yourself within the violet light of Love and compassion.

DAY 152: AND WHAT SHALL WE SPEAK OF TODAY?

And your Scribe asks, "And what shall we speak of today?" We speak of Love and experience the rapturous essence of Love. Our knowing and remembering of Love asks, "What of the absence of Love?" One cannot talk of Love without at the same time acknowledging the opposite side of the coin. Love's opposite is not-Love. Why do we speak of this? This is a time of inclusion; no part of creation is excluded. As all creation is divine expression, where there are only gradients of Love, the presence of Love is easy to see. What of the absence of Love? In the absence of Love the light presence is shallow, inhabited by more of not light. As we embrace all creation on equal footing we are within the structure of, and hold the key to, unity consciousness. As we stand in the light of Love, we hold space for the full expression of Love. It is easy to love Love. Is it easy to love not-Love?

The daily news contains events that are beyond reflections of political turmoil and are more representations of acts driven by not-Love. In your prayers are desperate requests and demands for the prevailing winds of Love to wipe all not-Love away. Instead, we say, All is Love. As you hold the high consciousness space of Love, instead of reacting, we ask you to consider applying the balm of Love to heal the chasm of consciousness.

As you hold strong the stance of Love, you begin to turn the tide, adding light where light was not before. As the fronts of not-Love are met in unseen realms, the application of Love is the balm that softens

94

barriers once hardened to the light. You too are on the edge of the revolution of Love. As you are beckoned to the edges of the expansive expression of Love that is you, your consciousness lends light and action to those corners of not light so they, too, may be restored. The imbalance on Gaia now reflects the inner revolution for the return to Love; an aligning with the divine essence that is the creation of Love.

As we move on the gradient scale of being, your awareness expands; the space you hold, the light you hold, has expanded exponentially. You are seen. You are known. You are embraced. The light you hold makes a difference far beyond your seeing of it. We ask you today to consider the scale of not only your expression but the scale of your contribution. Not only is the experience of your light adding to the Love, joy and freedom that is yours inherently, you also contribute light and healing to areas of creation that have not seen light. The areas of not light are areas of low consciousness that recoil in pain and have fallen so far, they no longer even hope for the rescue of Love. As you focus on all that *is* Love, you contribute to where it is not.

As your awareness expands, your light makes a difference. All the forces of light and Love stand united as a guard, ushering in the possibility for a new era of Love. As you BE Love during your moments, revel in the beauty, revel in the warmth of your divine expression. Know as you hold more and more of the light of Love that you are, you make a difference in areas you will never see. We hold a vast perspective. We see.

Cast Love, not fear. Your Love is a balm to All.

DAY 153: YOUR CALLING

*"There is no shortage of inspiration as we are willing to look beyond
the limitation of our beliefs."* —*Darlene*

Good morning. It is I, Thoth, stepping to the forefront of this
divine conversation taking place within this Now immaculate
moment. We as beings of light in light revel in each act of courage
as you move beyond perceived limitations of your past and step into
the light of what is possible. This is where your calling lies.

You have noticed a shift in tone of our work together. In our
collaboration now, the premise of our work together meets you at
your highest expression. We have moved focus from those qualities
and awareness that make a difference in your moments in form.
And now, as your divine expression in light has expanded, we meet
you in your light expression. Your expansive nature holds awareness beyond the experience in form you are most familiar with.
Understanding too, that the totality of you is contributed to with
each step in light expansion that is taken. Your physical experience
will continue to deepen and be enriched as your most expansive
Self finds voice with your conscious awareness. Each step you take
contributes to your totality.

The edges of your reality soften, revealing the chasm between
light and not light, Love and not-Love in stark contrast. Consider
that this is why you are reading these words within the matrix of *In
Service to Love.* You have longed for the aligning of the you in light
with the you in form, opening the floodgates to your highest vision

manifested. In your immaculate Now moments, your experience of Love's rapture holds many things. The treasure trove of your inspiration is but one.

Manifesting from the highest soul expression is more than a possibility; it occurs in each Now immaculate moment. The initial calling of your soul directs your attention and holds the space of your divine nature to be expressed. The Now immaculate moments reveal the creation. Times have changed since you incarnated. This too, was part of your plan. You hold the opportunity to apply the radical faith that draws you far beyond collective consciousness, into the realm of your highest expression made manifest. Your moments then reveal the more that is possible. Your calling awaits within your Now moments as you experience more of the Love that you are.

We direct your inquiries to what now is possible as your highest expression manifests in your physical reality. We suggest your capabilities lie far beyond that which was seen when you incarnated. This is the time you have been searching for. Your divine inspiration from your very essence is birthed into form at the spark of creation in the Now immaculate moment. Love is your new GPS. Your source of inspiration emanates from your divine essence in communication with your conscious awareness. You become a clear channel for you. You embody you at your highest expression.

Your Scribe has been experiencing just this, as she brings into form daily that which is inspired through divine collaboration. Your Scribe Darlene is in full participation. Without her, this expression of Love would not be possible.

Your divine expression awaits, lived in each magnificent Now moment. As you continue to release the limitations of your beliefs, the space is opened to embrace that which is your most deeply held truth. And you allow that to speak.

What could be possible?

Day 154: Potent Moments

G ood day. It is I, Thoth, stepping to the forefront of this divine conversation within this Now immaculate moment. Have I told you today how beautiful you are? I tell you again, how beautiful thou art. Your countenance is like no other. Your radiance inspires the greatest of poets, artists, and musicians. You emanate a celestial symphony with your smile.

As your expression in light emanates even more brilliantly, your experience in form resonates at higher and higher frequencies. The connection to the expression of you in light becomes more directly coupled in conscious awareness. In your day's moments, there is a new source of contribution. Your contributions in light to you in form are amplified. You are now more aware of innovative thoughts. New openings in your day's awareness are occurring. These openings are filled with the light of your highest expression. The light you are infuses your day's moments in even greater ways, seeming to expand daily. As you recognize the shifts in your perception, you hold the space open for potent moments to follow.

Potent moments are pivotal openings of potential. When recognized, a new expansive expression is realized. As you hold your space within the Now immaculate moment, you hold a powerful stance. It is an art form, one of mental discipline, orchestrated by your soul's desire for aligning expression. Understand that you are the conductor of these potent moments. They do not happen outside yourself. Your space of inspiration holds the canvas that is ready to respond to divine design in a moments flash. There is a moment where the artist places brush to canvas, moved to action by inspiration. These are potent moments.

As you encounter these potent moments, acknowledge them as responses to your highest expression. At times, this will also include inspiration from your divine team to you. Understand your divine team, as we with Darlene and you operate in response to your intentions, not ever overriding your thoughts, actions, or intentions. This morning Darlene asked us to meet her for our daily gathering; our response was swift. There is no time between the intention and our response. As we told Darlene, "As you are ready, we are here." First, Darlene must move toward us. That is our signal to engage. It is now a swift process. Previously laden with perceived patterns, rituals, and expectations. It is as simple as: You choose to go outside, so you open the door to the outside. Darlene sits at her computer and is ready to meet, so we meet. Or as she asks questions of us, and we respond, there is never an overriding of her intentions. We say this to remind you of the potency of you at your greatest expression.

The whole purpose of our work together is to support your connection increasingly with those beautifully poignant, soul satisfying, inspiring moments that are inherently you. Then, your highest expression that seeks voice may be heard. As you lend your voice to the heavenly symphony, or your color to the enraptured, swaying tide of creation, all creation is contributed to. Only *you* may be the expression of Love that you are. You are cherished as you are.

We remain,

In Service to Love

Day 155: The Expansive and Restorative Space of Innocence

There are many facets and layers to the expansion of conscious awareness. This is not a linear process. One principle may seem to contradict another. All are a part of the mystery. As the facets of you turn ever so gently, revealing new perspectives, different aspects of truth are revealed. Truth is so expansive that it may not even be spoken in its entirety. Finding your way through the process of conscious awareness is a path beset with paradoxes and incongruities. Today's conversation is one such example. Those present today contributing their light and signature energy to an ever-broadening perspective include Jeshua, Mary Magdalene, Isis, Buddha, St. Germain, Melchizadek, and Archangel Michael.

As your Scribe now sits with us, she waits for words to arise in her awareness. There is a space she reaches in her awareness that is neither relaxing meditation nor mental activity. It is a space of active receptivity. From this space there is no preselected thought, idea, or expectation. Just a being of openness at a high frequency range. As she sits, she waits. If words are not heard, she settles in more deeply into an active stance——of innocence.

From the space of innocence there is no agenda. Innocence only occurs within the Now immaculate moment. There are no edges representing past events, decisions, beliefs, and boundaries. There are no energies directed toward future planning; solely a presence in the vast expanse of innocence. Jeshua has said, "Come to me like a child." The reference is to the innocence of children not yet hardened or restricted by their belief systems, with access to their highest expression, remembering, and knowing.

Redefine your experience or sense of innocence. Innocence has a connotation of immaturity. In fact, the opposite is true. Innocence is so open to potential it resides at the flashpoint of creation. Innocence is the blank canvas of possibility. It holds a wisdom not tarnished with experience. It does not shy away in lack. Compassion, wholeness, and Love are inherently present within the state of innocence.

The Practice of Innocence as a Way of Being
Consider innocence a practice.

As you sit in the stillness, allow yourself to settle to a still point. In this still point is there any mental activity? View your thoughts as you would clothes hanging on a line to dry. As thoughts move into view, fold them like shirts and place them in a basket. Your breathing will slow. Gradually feel the expansive space of no-thing. The space of innocence holds no expectations, no history, no future, just Now. A space of observation. Feel the sense of openness that abides with innocence. Get a sense of the vast expanse that is present.

Feel the most positive expansive expression you can hold of innocence and be that. It is the space you occupied before you made your mind up. It is the space you held before something happened and you narrowed your view. As a child you held this deeply connected way of being. And then something happened, and the narrowing of your expression began. We ask you now, consciously, to remember the state of innocence and feel that now. This may be viewed as a restoration of a level of vitality that was held before there was a reflexive recoiling with pain. Moments spent in this expansive space are restorative. The calm that is present with this way of being opens avenues that were closed in reaction early in your life. Do you feel the shift?

As you practice holding this space for longer and longer periods of time you condition your being to that space. It is a space of high creativity. It is in the active state of innocence that your highest expression may speak to you.

In the process of *In Service to Love*, we find many ways to describe different states of being. The states of being we describe are distinct from your normal "get out of bed," "ready for the day," way of being. The states of being we describe bring you past the limitations of your day-to-day thinking, past the limitations of your beliefs and through resistance that may be created by your mind. All this to break through, so to speak, to a new way of being.

The state of innocence connects you with your vast expression. It is open and empty because the environment has not been judged or defined. It is an experience of "just is." And you are just you. As you sit in the space of your I AM, you connect with your most essential truth.

DAY 156: THE ADVOCACY OF LOVE

As in a house of mirrors, Love's reflections are distorted from the referencing they reside within. When the expectation of Love is to show up in a specific way, that then becomes the highest expression available. Your thoughts of Love are true. The limitations you hold of Love's embrace within the moments of your life are directly in alignment with your ability to see. When your experience of Love has been not-Love, or "good enough," or "just fine," there is an opportunity to see newly. A new perspective allows opportunity and space for a whole new range of possibilities. Stand way back and look at Love now.

With each step taken, Love advocates for your highest expression. Love waits patiently for you to release the thrashing experiences of not-Love. At the core of *In Service to Love*, we deliver the message that Love is here in each moment with you. As you are willing to release the limited views you have held of Love, the door opens for Love to be experienced unhindered. If your experience of Love has been not-Love, we gently urge you toward assuring yourself of the inner knowing you have always held deeply of Love's possibilities. As you release the sense of resignation, or "that is for some people but not for me," you realign with Love and the possibilities that are available within the high frequency experience of Love. The footsteps we take with you within the matrix of *In Service to Love* pave the way for a realigning with your greatest expression. When you are ready to shift your perspective, assuredly, new perspectives are available to be had. With each step toward Love you see more and more of the Love that has been waiting patiently within you, waiting for expression, waiting to be met. Waiting to be cherished.

Love is not a one-way street. Love is not earned. It is inherently who you are already. Finding your way back to your ultimate truth is the yellow brick road of the soul. The red slippers you wear align you with what you have always had. We would want you to see that the deep Love you hold within your heart, delivered unselfishly, completely, and hopefully to others in your life, is but one side of the coin. Turn to see the brilliant rays of warmth and safe harbor of Love. Love has already chosen you. Open the door again to experiencing the ease and softness of Love as Love awaits. Open the door again to the innocence. When the experience of Love has been so much of not-Love, it is easy to be hardened by the experiences in reflexive protection.

The Love we speak of does not require a relationship with anyone else. The Love we speak of is you meeting you at your highest expression of Love. We speak of you meeting you, in Love, then you move into a high-frequency relationship with yourself that is authentically you. As you choose Love as a way of being, by universal law, Love begets Love. As you meet you in the brilliance of Love's light, there is no space for not-Love.

As you meet your Self as the Beloved, your environment becomes the high-frequency expression of Love. And you *are* the Beloved. As Love surrounds you, then your Beloved in form finds you. It starts with you. Love is always advocating in your favor. Release the bonds of illusion to meet Love in real time. Now.

In Love,
With Love,
From Love,
The Council of Light

DAY 157: SHIFTING INTO EXPANSIVE AWARENESS

As you expand your awareness, the relationship to your physical environment moves. Your perspective is in continual motion.

In the process of expanding your conscious awareness, you have become more accustomed to a changing landscape. The reality of a changing environment has had you be aware of the distinctions between an experience of status quo informed by the past, and one created from your Now moments. Creations, thoughts, and actions within the Now contain a high level of potency. You have developed an adeptness in recognizing the qualities of your full presence in the moment in contrast with the lack of presence in your life. Your day reflects the access to clarity, wisdom, and broad perspective available through alignment with your I AM Self.

As you have embraced more of the light expression that you are, your base frequency has risen. Your relationship to everything has shifted. Moving within your day contains a new experience, identified as different from "before." Your awareness is now more expansive. You no longer hold a myopic view of your day's events and the people that you interact with. You bring a larger expression of you to your day. You are seen. Beyond the awareness of most, you notice your shifting connection with people. An opening is present perhaps where one did not exist before. A softness in the eyes as you pass each other, a kind compassionate interchange as you go about the day, reflect the new depth that is available.

The reduction of reactivity to your life identifies a new viewpoint. The myopic limitations are now somehow diluted. You have added new notes to your repertoire. The opus you play has depth, clarity, and resonance of harmony as you are more light filled. Almost as in a dream, the density of your memories fades. You will not see them in the same way.

Your shifting awareness requests a continual aligning as you get used to an expanding reality. From the perspective of your human nature, what you had been seeking was the assurance that all you knew was right. Now, in the light of your light-filled, expansive, divine nature, you hold space for you to be present from your highest possibility. You see an ebb and flow of your awareness during the day. The difference shows up in the increasing moments of exalted knowing. The resonance of truth embraces every cell of your being. Being right pales in comparison with being Love, or joy, or peace, or clarity or whatever you choose, from the Now.

We know that ease within an ever-changing landscape may seem elusive, as your awareness is pulled to new ways of thinking and experiencing. As you occupy more of you, there is so much more to see. You are processing much more in your day's moments. You already know how to do this. In the space of inquiry, all is fluid as you utilize your expansive awareness aligned with your I AM Self.

Rest when you need to rest. Your vitality exists in the Now moment. Consider being gentle and compassionate with yourself. The process of conscious awareness works on you as you seek it. The joy and the peace of this process resides within a broad perspective. The edges of reality soften as you move in light.

DAY 158: CROSSING THE BARRIER TO AWARENESS

We could endlessly produce information and concepts around the expansion of consciousness and actualization. It would take lifetimes, and we still would not run out of material. But producing the information, analogies, examples, and shifts in perspectives is only as good as their employment. The words we utilize through the scribing process are infused with frequency that supports you in the process of expansion. Specific topics and days have included opportunity for mighty shifts in energetic awareness. Today we speak of what it takes to live the reality of expanded conscious awareness.

Your perspective has shifted. The human mind has a capability of handling only so much change before an automatic governor steps in and controls the input. Have you felt that at work in your experience? Human nature is naturally reactionary. When the shock of reaction enters your reality, you stop all higher functions and move to survival. Your physiology shifts as well. Breathing gets shallow, attention is piqued. This is the fight-or-flight way of being. There was a time when reaction would save your life, as in early civilizations. Now, in your technologically driven world, your awareness level is at a peak most of the time. You have an input of streaming information with you always. Your technology keeps you connected 24/7. It takes an effort now to move *out* of reaction.

There is a process of polarization that is occurring. The power is on for survival, and then when you have time to think of it, power is turned on for consciousness. As we contribute concepts, light infusions, and activations in support of your unique process of enlightenment, you find your human nature is gradually integrated with your divine nature. The natural compartmentalization of your life will yield to the high resonance of your broadest perspective as your awareness is present in the moment. Increasing your awareness of reflexive reaction increases the opportunity for conscious choice.

Circumvent Reaction and Respond

The way we may circumvent the natural process of compartmentalization is through observing it. When you find yourself in a reaction, as in, "I only have a short window of time to get a project completed," or "I have friends who are in crisis," or "I am in crisis," or "I just saw the news," begin to train your brain to register differently. Utilize reaction now as a red flag for shifting your awareness. Breathe first. Then acknowledge you are in reaction.

Utilize reactionary moments as a red flag to signal your choice for a broader perspective. As you choose to raise your frequency in response *to a situation, you automatically employ your highest awareness. You are declaring who you BE in the moment. It's much more powerful and workable than having reaction shut you down and escalate the perceived problem.*

As you acknowledge the automatic experience of reaction, you are no longer controlled by it. You choose a new way to view the situation. A broader perspective available through your own divine nature offers fine frequency access to resolution.

Observe reaction
Reaction is:
   —Lightning fast
   —Sourced from either the past or the future

Neutralize reaction
   —Breathe, "I will do this differently now."

—Remove assessments from the past or future.

—Focus on the Now moment.

Access broader perspective

—Raise your frequency.

—Access your higher knowing by declaring who you BE. "I choose clarity, I choose Love, I choose peace, I choose integrity," and so on.

Respond

—The response will be sourced beyond limitations of reaction.

—Open the door to possibility you haven't seen before.

—Allow clarity to be revealed. It takes a few moments. Reaction is lightning fast. Responding considers. Allow response to arise within you.

—Your response will hold resonance.

As you develop the "muscles" to look at reaction from an empowered perspective, you are in fact opening new neural pathways. Instead of shutting down in those moments of perceived need, you access your full capacity. Your broad perspective will see the situation beyond the emotional constrictions. Resolution will be sourced by your highest expression.

The pace of your technologically driven world provides many advantages and hinders many of the natural capacities you have as well. Our work together will continue to support your highest expression on all levels. What is now possible when you bring all of you to bear in life?

DAY 159: REACHING FOR YOUR NEXT STATE OF AWARENESS

Your greatest work is a moment away. In the search for your greatest expression, there are the patterns and ways of being that are human nature to be considered. In the same way as there is a governor that slows down information you receive in order to stay within the realm of known, there is an internal process that will always and reliably direct you toward your comfort. This is where the distinction between your human nature and your divine nature meet.

Your own unique process of enlightenment is the process whereby you surpass perceived limitations of your human nature to integrate your divine nature. Previously thought separate and perhaps even unattainable, your divine essence is the part of you urging you on to see beyond the veil of illusion to what else may be possible. It is the perfectly timed signal from your divine essence that is calling you forth. Your inner quest for something you don't know but can sense is the beginning. As you hold the door open for that which resides beyond your known physical world, you live in the realm of possibility where your wholeness may be actualized. The greatest expression of your wholeness is enlightenment; the full integration of your human nature and your divine nature as your fundamental way of being.

Your human nature will react, searching for sameness within the known realm. Discomfort within the unknown is to be expected.

Guided now by the resonance available in the moment, and directed by your divine nature your next steps are assured, and the discomfort of your human nature is no longer a limitation.

The challenge for your human nature is the reality of trusting an expanding perspective that is informed no longer by your past but by your essential Self in the present moment. Choosing to reach beyond the limitations of your human nature honors who you are in your totality. As you embrace your authentic expression you allow the light of Love to be your beacon. These are patterns of mastery.

DAY 160: ALL

The connection you hold with all creation becomes clear as you gain the broad perspective afforded you through your divine essence. You are a contribution to the All. In the same way one drop of water contributes to the oceans, so are you to the creation of All. Your individual, specific expression is integral and inseparable from the whole. Unique in your expression, the depth, quality, and expanse of your moments contributes not just to your life and those close to you, but to All.

The purpose of this conversation is the energy that it holds in support of the expansion of your awareness. As you begin to consider yet again who you are, consider looking beyond the compartmentalization of human nature.

Your truth lies beyond the limitations of your thinking. As you engage your divine nature your expectations soften and you live within the realm of possibility that allows you to peer through the veil of illusion. Your awareness gains dimensionality; gradually you perceive what is not seen. You will begin to perceive the between moments. As you interact with all facets of your being, notice the tendency to compartmentalize areas you understand as separate from the nonlinear aspects of your essential Self. When you can begin to see your Self as your human nature, your divine nature, and your interconnectedness with All, you hold a broad perspective allowing you to see the vistas of your truth.

The presence of unity consciousness invites your awareness of All. As you see yourself and experience yourself as All, you are connecting not only with your highest expression in a way that is nonlinear, but with your own wholeness. As you embrace your wholeness, you hold the door open for the integration of your divine nature as your reality now, with ease and grace.

DAY 161: HEARING YOUR OWN VOICE

As awareness of your divine nature increases in depth and breadth, the lines that are the division between your human expression and your divine expression are softened. In response to your request to see with more clarity, we speak of a new way to communicate with your I AM Self.

You feel the calming presence of your divine nature with more clarity now. You feel a natural flow in your life and can easily identify more clearly when that is not present. We move now to fine-tune your natural abilities to an even greater extent. The space you step into holds a sense of fine awareness. The feeling is expansive with no sense of boundaries. The experience is a bit disorienting, as you step into a new dimensional understanding. The space you find yourself at now exists in the outer reaches of your conscious awareness. Your Scribe now is having an experience of broadened awareness she is trying to understand. She finds herself pulling up a chair within this new space and sitting there to get reoriented. You have crossed over a threshold of awareness into a new vast space where the interrelationships you have known are fine, more "delicate," informative, vivid, resonant, and experiential.

You have crossed over a threshold of awareness. Thresholds hold powerful imagery as they place a distinction between what was previously available and a new space that has opened. The new space has opened because you hold the resonant tone that is the key for the next stage to unlock before you. As you move forward, as you choose, of course, beyond the threshold, you get a sense of more space. The space is filled with sounds, colors, imagery, and sensing that holds information. There is not a feeling of the solidity of "things." This is an expansive space of sensing and resonant experience.

If you walk in your garden and you see a rose, utilizing your normal sensing, you see a rose, you smell the rose, you see the colors of the petals, the size of the plant, you sense the vitality and season. While in the heightened state of awareness that is available in the new space which has now opened, a whole new range of information is available. Utilizing this expanded, deepened sensing, you would see the rose before you and then see the whole history of the plant from its original inception. You would feel the experience of the rose through each season of its expression. You would feel the vitality. You would see the original design, potential, and actualization of the rose. All available within a moment. This heightened information is available within the new space that has opened before you. Not as a space you live in, but as a space you may now choose to experience and gather information within. There is the equivalent of this information that is available about you. You may experience you in light and gather information from this high resonant field. If you choose to learn about the you that resides in light, you go to the frequency where that information is located.

You may choose to move to this space to hear your voice more clearly. The space that has just opened is of fine enough frequency that it holds the potential for connection.

Invitation into a Space of Clarity

We invite you to this space of expanded awareness. There is no doing within this space. This space of expanded connection invites only your being. We invite you to come and pull up a chair and sit down to feel the space you have just moved into. From the observation mode, we ask you to consider listening from the context of being. When you utilize an expanded state of being to sense your new environment, you are more of a match for what is available within this new rarefied space.

Take a deep breath and be. See what you see, feel what you feel. If you were sitting across the table from your most expanded Self that resides in light, what might you hear? Allow the space to speak to you. This is a space of Love.

Who you are is cherished. Who you are is profoundly beautiful. Allow the extraordinarily rich space before you to come to you. Today we Be.

DAY 162: THE QUALITIES OF YOUR AWARENESS

B eyond the threshold, within the lightness of the new space now revealed, your awareness has expanded as well. The period of adjustment has been akin to being in a loud concert, then immediately stepping into a whisper-quiet environment. Moving from one environment to another requires a few moments of adjustment as your sensory abilities settle down and align with the finely tuned information now available.

You have developed a pattern of being and sensing during your day that is automatic and resides beneath your conscious awareness. Your awareness is tuned to the level needed to get done what you need to get done in your day. As particular situations require a higher level of consideration, you have made the necessary adjustments to accommodate the need. Through the access to this now fine space, the quality of your awareness capacity has increased. Consider the shift as fine-tuning the focus on a camera. There is a normal focus function you utilize regularly. When there are special situations, conditions, or effects, a higher degree of clarity may be required. Your expanded awareness may be viewed as the new lens for your camera that provides a greater clarity and sensitivity than normal. In other words, you now have a lens for that.

The high level of sensitivity of your new awareness will be providing input for you in a variety of ways. You have a capacity to hear more, feel more, sense more, see more. You may direct attention toward the level of awareness you have always had, but now you hold a higher level of discrimination that always operates on your behalf. You may experience this expanded awareness as clarity, greater insight, and intuition.

Another way to access this space is through your ability to BE. Your beingness will absorb the information beyond your ability to think it. This sensing activates your processing of light beyond your ability to understand. You perceive through sensing within this environment, then your mind will attempt to interpret it after the fact. If you choose to stay in the mode of being while you are in this rich space, a whole new range of information will be made available, before your mind has a chance to label it.

Access Beyond the Threshold

How do you then consciously experience this space that is beyond your thinking of it?

First, visualize yourself stepping over the threshold and finding a comfortable place to sit.

Just feel the space around you. With the intention of curiosity, be still and feel. Just be. Do you sense the light in the air? Do you sense symbols or colors?

Your awareness has expanded. Move to a space of inquiry and curiosity in your day. Do you notice you are perceiving more?

The capacity your awareness holds is awe inspiring. We delight in each new discovery of the abilities you have always held.

DAY 163: ANCHORING THE LIGHT

The vast space before you is a space you navigate naturally. Although new to your human awareness, your divine nature navigates light effortlessly. You naturally know how to distill the information and communication that is available and anchored in this environment.

The space feels vast and fine; perhaps a little light-headed sensation is experienced. When your mind reads the writing from a few days ago announcing you have newly accessed this space, your mind will go into questioning. "I'm not sure that has happened for me." We assure you, your reach into this space is available. The new component of this accessibility is your awareness of it. This represents a gathering of more of the light that you are authentically into your awareness. Consider that your ability for finer sensing within a broader perspective is ever present, providing information beyond your usual sensing ability. The expanded access of awareness will be revealed in a variety of ways throughout your day. You will find moments of deeper connection, clarity, and satisfaction. Joy and peace are experienced at deeper levels. The feeling of "baggage" of the past has less of a hold on you. New options of empowerment are seen. "Dreams" may include consciousness downloads. You may see glints of light in your periphery. Moments of inspiration are increasing. In general, there is a softer sense of your being. All this is due to you accessing the greater part of your expression that resides in light. All this is attainable through the conduit of the Now moment.

Your access of this space has been previously unconscious. The experience may be compared with owning a home that is 500,000 square feet in size, but you have lived in only 2,000 square feet of it. One day you discover a hallway and a door that when opened reveals a magnificent ballroom. You have owned the ballroom, as a part of the home, but are just now just getting to enjoy the beauty that has been there all along.

Your conscious awareness of this space anchors the light that you are naturally. As you take conscious ownership you amplify your divine expression. This is the natural integration of your human nature with your divine nature.

Within this space you perceive fine frequencies. As you align your conscious awareness to a new subtle sensing, you will begin to see slight shifts. Consider that your "coarse" normal daily awareness is being finely tuned to perceive a broad range of frequencies. It is here in this fine space of light that is you that you may gather communication from your highest expression. From this fine environment you absorb information and experience in the same way a rose would process light. It is a natural flow of your expression, received differently. You are not utilizing the five senses needed for physical life. There is another fine sense that is moving to the forefront.

Words may only convey so much. We choose to paint a picture with the words that allow you to look at the more diffuse expressions of you from a new perspective.

Who you are naturally is extraordinary. Our work together is intended to bring your conscious awareness to who you already are. We hold the space of clarity as you connect with what you have always known.

DAY 164: ALIGNING WITH YOUR LIGHT

The rich expanded range of frequency you have entered offers a conduit for clear communication between the you in form and the you in light. This is a space you have inhabited mostly unconsciously as your light expression has always been informing your human nature. Beyond the density of your humanity lies your divinity. Enlightenment is a process of expanding consciousness where your access to the potent realm of your I AM Self becomes the new beacon lighting the direction of your life. In order to reach this rich field of light, your willingness to look beyond beliefs and the density of your past opens the door to full alignment with your essential Self. All that is yours to be, do, and have is no longer met with resistance from your human nature, and you may create the opus of your life informed consciously by your I AM Self.

Keen Awareness

As you occupy more and more light consciously, your sensitivities, thoughts, and actions shift to hold more of the light you are. It is for this reason we ask you to consider how finely tuned your awareness is.

As you sit in meditation or your specific practice, visualize a dial before you. The dial amplifies or reduces your level of sensitivities. Like turning up the volume on your signature energy (the frequency pattern signal that identifies you as you), you may utilize this visualization to amplify your level of keen awareness to align with the fine space you have just stepped into, understanding you are aligning with your divine nature of Love. You may choose to turn the dial up a bit to amplify your awareness within this space.

As you amplify your awareness or range of perception, you are naturally expanding the range of your conscious reach. You will notice the increase in information you receive. At first it may feel a little surprising.

As you hold the stance of observing, the more time you spend in this potent space, the more this potent space of Love and light works on you. For example, a fish in the environment of water is wet. A cat sleeping in the environment of sunlight is warm. You, consciously aligning with light, are imbued with the qualities that reside in light. The environment you are within acts upon you, whether dense or light filled.

You each have your unique ways of connecting and gathering information; some are more auditory, kinesthetic, visual, or verbal. Look to what you already know about the way you incorporate information to get clues for how information may be gleaned within this high-frequency space. And then look beyond what you know to find the unique actions of this space.

The context you held of environment before does not apply. Environment implies an inside and an outside. What if you were one with the environment? What if there were no definitive edges? If you are immersed in the light of Love, what becomes available?

DAY 165: THE NATURALLY EXPANSIVE ORDER OF CREATION

The opportunity at hand today is integration of the light expression you are into your awareness consciously. There have been four days of acclimation into this space since it was introduced. The opportunity at hand is a claiming of your highest knowing. This is a part of your natural expansion of awareness. This access may be likened to the acknowledgment and appreciation of a new expression in life, such as maturing into womanhood and manhood. This is a natural expansion or evolution of creation. As all creation continually evolves and expands, so too does your awareness and the expression of your I AM presence.

This space of Love is the conduit for clarity of communication with your highest expression. The environment is fine, filled with light, Love, and creative potential. This is where your authentic, most potent expression resides. The energetic matrix offered today supports further integration of your divine awareness with your daily conscious awareness. This provides a new vast perspective from which to live your life, with less resistance to who you are at your greatest expression.

What this means for your physical expression is a new infusion of light and an expanded awareness. The frequency of your awareness will shift to a higher range. Rather than the events of your day running through the evaluation process of your human nature, the opportunity present has the moments of your days run through the fine filters of your highest expression in light. The ease of being in the moment becomes your new default. The access to your knowing and authentic expression at the highest of levels will be integrated more easily. This is a process of infusion. As the rose processes light, so do you. Along with this infusion available today is the unique application of the impulse of light received with ease and grace by all your systems.

Divine Infusion of Light

There are many divine beings of light in light present, that as you, are a stand for Love throughout creation. The space opening is acknowledged as sacred. You are honored as the divine expression of Love that you are. This is a momentous occasion, a celebration of ushering you into a new level of light expression.

The space has been prepared. As you choose to participate, your wishes are abided. The infusion will begin as you are ready. Motion may be felt at your crown chakra. This action in light connects the high frequencies of your expression in light, making available the wisdom of your soul.

This process meets you where you are. If you are not at the point to fully assimilate the light that is being made available, it is held for you in your field, until such time as you choose. Your highest expression is always the gatekeeper. For some this is an immediate process, for others it will be occurring over time.

The feeling may be like having lived in an environment that is dull, only noticed as you begin to see with new clarity. The brilliance of colors and the rich subtleties that escaped your awareness previously now come into view. The communication between you in light and you in form is enhanced and moves at the speed of light, seamlessly. This is already who you are. You have been heard. The mission and intention of your soul holds a potent expression. This action in access to light supports the mission of your soul, beyond boundaries of physical limitation. The divisions between the dimensional expressions of you are fine. Previously perceived as impenetrable walls, they are now viewed as diaphanous veils of light.

This infusion action is now complete. Know you have received that which is yours to receive.

The lotus petals open in the expansive process of enlightenment revealing the illumined beauty of truth. This is witnessed by many and celebrated beyond the central sun. It is with joy and appreciation we acknowledge the contribution you are.

DAY 166: MORE OF WHO YOU ARE

I am here, Beloved. It is I, Thoth, stepping to the forefront of this divine conversation within this Now immaculate moment. There are many ways in which we, the Masters of your Council of Light, communicate. Transmitting to you as you sit before your computer screen is but one. We connect as you are in the Now moment in awe of the beauty surrounding you. We connect in music you hear. The Love songs are our words to you. We relay Love in the magic moments that touch your heart. There are no limits to the expression of Love. All to remind you of your truth.

The expression of you in light requests your attention toward your *being* within your day. It is in the Now immaculate moment that your voice may be heard with clarity. The expressions of Love that you experience are the authentic moments of your highest expression communicating to you. Love transforms.

The vast space of light and high frequency you have conscious access to holds a depth of expression and awareness that resides beyond words. Words alone may not relay the full message. Light, frequency, and resonance carry the new potent communications available. As you focus attention toward who you BE in the moment, you have access to clarity beyond the limited assessment and protocol of your mind. Focusing on who you Be, requires making the distinction between moments when you are choosing to BE joy, clarity, peace, and Love, and those moments when there is an absence of conscious awareness. Can you identify when you are sourced by a default way of being that is led by your mind? As you focus your awareness on who it is you Be, your choice declares powerfully how your day goes. As you choose from an empowered perspective, you access the part of you that holds elevated and expansive knowing. This is a process of expanding conscious awareness. Declaring who you BE, daily, is a significant component of that process.

Choosing who you BE occurs within the Now immaculate moment and focuses your awareness to the clarity available only Now.

So far, you have seen reflections of your highest expression. As you set the intention to access the clarity that is naturally you, you begin to see who you are, fully empowered, as a magnificent, unique expression of Love. Your hearing adjusts to the finely tuned capacity needed to hear the voice of your soul. Your moments are attuned to receive direction and clarity from your most potent self. The Love you experience in your moments is informed by the vast being of Love that you are.

Bask in the spaciousness of your being. Hear the voice of your soul in unison with Masters on high.

Day 167: To What Do You Assign Power?

Today we speak of the ability you hold authentically, beyond comprehension of your human nature. When one is Source extended into form, to whom do you look for answers?

We assert there are areas of your life, thinking, patterns, and beliefs where you assign power beyond yourself. This is a function that is so automatic to human nature that it is a subconscious activity. Today, we shine light on those areas so you may realign with your innate divine expression.

Over the last week or so, an opening has been created within your conscious awareness of the vast space that you occupy. We have spoken of the infinite knowledge that is available to you through your own unique divine expression. At this point we would like to direct your attention to those situations where you automatically direct power to others beyond yourself. If what we are doing together in our divine collaboration is supporting your access to the most expansive, infinite qualities of your being, we suggest you reconsider, when in moments of habit, you assign power beyond your own nature. This includes us, your divine team in light. We have asked you to consider taking your place at the table and be with us from the perspective of eye to eye, peer to peer, divine to divine. We invite you to be present with all aspects of your being from the potent Now immaculate moment. Activities are suggested, all in support of revealing a new way of being, sourced by the Love that you are.

Unless you identify those moments that defer empowerment to others, the avenues created with our work together are empty halls, and potential remains in light. Very early on, we asked you to consider cutting the cords and ties with past situations that held your power encased in the past. The immaculate Now moment is the unencumbered access to creating that which is informed by your highest expression. Where do you dilute the richness of your ability by looking elsewhere for qualities that are your nature?

That which you imbue with power is in fact imbued with the power you give it. Books, crystals, teachers, healing methods, enlightened practices, Masters both in light and in form, inspired works such as this, may all direct your attention back to you, reflecting your innate abilities, possibilities, and potential. The high frequency of masterful work resonates with you not because it may outline a path for your growth and give you something to aspire to, but because it resonates with your essential truth.

Utilize resonance to turn your attention newly toward your expansive, divine, unique, exquisite expression. Anything less is a "power-over" and "power-under" type of relationship and the results will contain the limitations of separation consciousness. Allow inspiration to catalyze your clarity within.

We ask once more, "When one is Source in form, to whom do you look for answers?"

Day 168: Looking Ahead

B eloveds, today's conversation is related to the concept of looking for answers within the integrity of your own divine nature.
As you have moved more deeply into the light expression that is
your divine domain, the gauge utilized for evaluation has shifted
as well. We suggest that any evaluation and tools of assessment that
you utilize at this point are garnered from your past. They are fil-
tered through your mind and based on the assessment of better,
more, farther, to determine your place and movement made in your
growth. We are suggesting the new space you have access to holds a
plethora of new ways to sense your movement. Look in front of you,
ahead, toward your most expanded light expression for answers.

The vast space you have always had access to is your authentic expression reflecting your divine nature. It holds realms of
information delivered, processed, and accessed at the speed of
light. Can you feel that the old ways of assessing and evaluating
moments of your day belonged to a way of being that you held
from the perspective of your human nature and the inherent
limitations? Unless you are consciously employing your unlimited
divine nature, your physical experience is evaluated through the
limitations of your past. Now that you are manifesting consciously,
within an environment that is based in light, your access to and
receipt of information is processed in a fashion that matches your
light expression.

Now, as you create space to connect with your highest expression, beyond the busy activity of your day, you call forth all parts of

your being that reside in light. There is a transfer of types of information expressed through light. The light holds within it a depth of experience and expression that is beyond your mind's understanding of it but is the vehicle of your soul's essential Self.

As you are reading this, we embrace you in light. Do you feel the caress of light around your shoulders? This is an example of a communication in light. Beyond touch, there is a conveyance of light and Love, catalyzing clarity of your next moments. There is and always has been a whole broad band of expression residing in light that, like the background of silence holding the note of a violin's string, holds your essential expression in the immaculate Now moment, awaiting divine infusion of creation; awaiting your choice.

DAY 169: CONNECTION

Your connection to All that you are resides in the Now moment. There is no "trying" to connect; you are *always* connected. You are merely refining the method to move information available in light past the mechanics and brilliance of your mind. The exquisite wealth of information, potential, and alchemy that you hold is infinite. Your uniqueness lies, too, in the fact that there are few who ask the questions you ask.

Today we ask you to consider your perspective when you choose to reach more deeply into the expression of you that resides in light. When you stand at the less-enlightened end of the spectrum and ask for connection you are limited by the constraints of the frame of reference you hold within the question. The perspective held by your human nature says, "I want that," as opposed to "I AM that." Do you feel the difference? Your perspective is informed by the state of consciousness you hold when you ask. When you hold the perspective of owning fully that which you are, there is a natural flow of expression that is highly creative and potent.

Move to the space of being fully enlightened, aligned with your I AM Self. Place yourself in the space of knowing all there is to know, and then ask. There are natural barriers to be crossed when you broach the topic of connecting with the infinite from the perspective of being a "mere mortal."

As we move further afield within the expanded dynamic of our divine collaboration your perspective will continually be asked to be refined. When you move into a space of inquiry and expectation of your highest, most expanded Self, showing up, *you do*. Equally, when you hold the perspective of what you already know, as you ask, whatever you receive may only be perceived through the lens of limitation and nothing new will be seen. The enlightenment process is the integration of your human nature and your divine nature. Holding this broad perspective is helpful as you make choices in your life.

DAY 170: IMPRESSIONS

The rich spaces of frequency now available to you consciously are experienced as environments, not things, necessarily easily identified. You are now beginning to sense the space that resides between things.

When you step into a new environment that is different from that which you recognize as normal, there is a realigning that takes place as you assess the qualities of your surroundings. The way to best relay this is through experiences you have already had. Identify a time when you traveled far from your home.

Darlene is now on the opposite coast of the United states. When the plane landed, immediately a difference was detected. Not in the airport, but in the environment. It no longer felt like the familiarity of home. She observes what she does with the experience.

When you land in a new space, the environment gives you information beyond the things you see. You get a sense of the history of the environment. You feel a difference in culture. You recognize the people there as having a different sense of being from what you are used to. A rich space of information unfolds before you. The things are still there—beach, people, buildings, restaurants—but the experience feels new. This is what we are relaying about your experience within a new range of light frequencies.

The information is revealed to you through impressions. Impressions relay what words cannot. The environment speaks to you and gives you information and experience. Consciousness is delivered to you through impressions.

Impressions are formulations of light, coding, and consciousness that when received reveal depth, sensory information, sound, color, dimension, and history. Impressions communicate a rich tapestry of experience, beyond what words may convey from 3D experience. As you move your awareness through the gradients of light into the finer levels of expression, your depth and range of perception is keen. You gather information through the environment you are in. You allow the space you are in to speak to you. It's not unlike our communications with Darlene as she scribes.

Natural Ability

As you inquire about your experiences in light, look to your history and recall how you felt when you traveled abroad. Once you arrived, how did you gather information? How did you adapt to the new space? There is a process that occurred before you adapted that we shine the light upon. How did you assess information about your new environment? How did that information come to you?

Consider that you were utilizing your ability to process light information. You gathered information from the collective consciousness of the area through impressions. We ask you to consider focusing on your natural ability to adapt. Adapting comes from assessing and then placing what you see within the new environment into a template you are familiar with. Before you adapt you assess, automatically.

The process of expansion of consciousness utilizes the ability to assess through impressions that are received. Instead of placing the information into a template of a known experience, the door is left open for a new way of being to show up expressing the specifics of that range of light. Impressions are an expansive, multidimensional experience. You process information from light all the time. You just don't recognize it as such. Start looking for ways you already process information that occurs beyond your identification of things. Develop an awareness of the subtlety of impressions.

Your divine essence already communicates to you through the prism of limitations of your human nature. As you release the resistance of limitations seen through your human nature, you will find that impressions hold depth and richness beyond the capacity of words.

There is music floating in the air, and rich history emanating from the cobblestones. Allow the air of your environment to gift you.

DAY 171: EMANATE

All nature holds a life force; the essential energy that holds the specifics of the divine design of the creation. For example, trees hold a life force that may be seen at times as an aura or white halo of light around them. The auras of people may also be detected by those who are becoming sensitive to finer light frequencies. If you can visualize the concept of auras and the information they hold, you may begin to understand the concept of emanation.

You emanate not only the life force you hold but the particulars of your own exquisite expression, like your signature energy that identifies you as you within all creation. You, as a divine expression of Source, are the origin of the emanations of light you emit. As you pass by someone you automatically read information about who they are by sensing their emanations. Information gleaned through sensing the light of others is an action that is mostly unconscious until such time as you entertain yourself as more than mortal.

The emanations of light you emit are increasingly expanded in scope, clarity, and alchemical qualities, reflecting the level of conscious awareness held. As with the polishing of a diamond at one time buried below the surface of the earth, with care and attention the diamond's true qualities are revealed, allowing light to be reflected through each facet. As you gain conscious awareness of the scope of your divine expression, you emanate the light of your highest essence unhindered. Beliefs, actions, and consciousness in contradiction to your essential Self, your I AM Self, dampen and somewhat skew the clarity of the light you emit.

When your beingness, consciousness, and actions align with the highest expression of your divine design, the light you emanate holds an alchemical ability to transform and create. When your human nature is aligned with your divine nature, the clarity and brilliance of your being cuts through darkness like a knife. You, as Love, transform.

Who you are is Source extended into form.

DAY 172: THE POWER OF LOVE

A s you allow Love to be your GPS, you are automatically connected with high-frequency presence in the Now moment.

One of the distinctions of Love is its magnetic quality. Love is
your greatest tool for manifestation. As you become a beacon for
Love, all that is in alignment with your highest expression is drawn
into your field. Love moves that which resides within the field of
potentiality into form. Have you noticed resources moving into
your field? Not just money, but right people appearing at the right
time in so-called coincidences. The universe does not distinguish
between small or big and does not award or bestow. The magnetic
quality of Love is an action in response to your being. As you align
with your highest expression, a natural quality is not only the experience of more Love, but the access to more of what resides naturally in your field. Who you are is naturally abundant in all areas of
your life. As you focus on living from the perspective of being and
owning your divine nature, there is a natural flow of abundance in
your field.

One of the qualities that separates your abundance from you is
the condition of wanting or holding abundance separately. If abundance is held in a field that has it be separate from you, as in, "I
want it, but I don't have it," or "how can I get it, because I don't have
it," there is a repulsion in effect. Like two magnetic fields in opposition. Do you see that? We recommend that you consider the stance
of holding your abundance in your field, as in, you ARE abundance
on all levels. In the same way you relate to the color of your eyes

and your height; you naturally ARE. As you hold the perspective of your divine nature you naturally release resistance to all that is yours. You, as Love, connected with All, have no limits. Resist the condition of wanting and migrate toward already owning. Practice the act of receiving. Receive the light and warmth from the sun. Receive the Love and friendship from those around you. Notice your limiting beliefs around abundance and re-choose. Stand in the light of Love and say Yes! The being of Love catalyzes a powerful alchemical process.

Open the front door and allow all the abundance you hold in your field to come flowing in. Look who you already have as mentors, teachers, and advocates for your divine expression! What else could be possible?

DAY 173: LOVE AS YOUR WAY OF BEING

R est assured this is indeed a conversation. We are with you throughout this process. It is your being that speaks to us. We hear all levels of your being as a request for clarification to be made.

There are moments in the expansion of consciousness when new levels are reached; today is one such day. Velocity of expansion has expanded to embrace a new gear. What this means is that there is a new freedom that is available within the experience of *In Service to Love*. As you express your highest level of awareness in your day's moments, you are being sourced from a new, more expansive space of your awareness. The expansion of your awareness paves the way for what is to come, as new levels of light are accessed.

There is a new opening for the being of Love as a flowing, natural experience. Not one that needs to be thought of, manipulated into your awareness, or identified as different. The space opening at this moment allows the receipt of a greater level of divine light awareness. This appears in your life's moments both as clarity around what is preferable and clarity around what is not preferable. The identification of preference is valuable as empowering choice. The space of being that you are moving into is one that is no longer fueled by the past; instead it is a level of awareness that is fueled by Love available in the moment. Consider that your fuel source has shifted away from the limitations of past referencing and external referencing to the availability of being Love as a natural choice present in the moment.

The more moments you BE Love within your day, the more you notice a new reality arise. Your experience reflects the expansive, heart-warming, and soul-satisfying resonance of your truth. Being Love is a natural choice, residing in the background of your awareness. As the experience of ease is realized through being Love, the propensity to be Love increases. Each moment now becomes more vibrantly alive with sensing, appreciation, Love, joy, clarity, and possibility.

We support and facilitate, as you choose, the function of integrating to a new range of frequency. The light you emanate is a brilliant contribution to All.

DAY 174: THE VOICE OF YOUR SOUL

A s it becomes easier to place aside those things that are not you, the perfection of your exquisite nature is revealed.

Beyond the thoughts, beyond the judgments, beyond the external cues, reside the hallowed halls of your sacred expression. The process within *In Service to Love* beckons you down the hallowed halls to more clearly hear the voice of your essential Self.

Your essential Self exists beyond incarnations, beyond physical form and physical influences. Your sacred expression is timeless and formless. You are Source. When you move through the maze of physical expression, you allow the physical world to be a contribution to your experience rather than limit or define you. Your greatest expression becomes manifest as you integrate the light of your divine nature and align with the fine frequency of your I AM Self. Throughout this process of awakening and enlightenment you develop a clear, unhindered connection to your highest expression so your soul's voice may be heard.

As you hear the clarion call of your soul's expression, your human experience is elevated. You move deftly, with clarity and delight, emanating the perfection of you. You bridge realities, contributing to All. Your expansive divine nature is magical, alchemical, and sourced by Love.

The voice of your soul holds the keys to the "more" you have yearned for. This is the time you have been waiting for. Your time is Now. We are with you in Love, support, gratitude, and unity. We join our voices in the name of Love for the benefit of All. Your I AM is that magnificent.

DAY 175: THE JOY OF BEING

When you experience being Love, there is no situation that feels separate. You are informed by a vast perspective.

As the attunement of your awareness expands, you notice subtleties previously hidden from view. Your expanded sensitivity is a quality that enhances your life. You hold a broad range of expression. The days of holding a highly sacred space of holiness upon the mountaintop are no longer helpful. The ability to weave the light of your divine nature into your life is what transforms.

For example, your Scribe is at a beach setting with country music playing within a party atmosphere. She chuckles as there is no loss of potency in our connection. Bringing all of you to the moment expands your experience.

As you choose the being of Love as a background for your day, the edges of judgment diminish. You find that openness, freedom, and appreciation reigns. Judgment is replaced with observation that is free of labels. The generosity of heart applied to your Self in the process of releasing limiting belief systems is now available in relation to others. Your new way of being from the perspective of unity consciousness translates into your days. The automatic separation expressed through thoughts and beliefs is no longer in alignment with who you are. You will notice separation becomes a foreign response. As you embrace unity consciousness, your ability to relate to others and extend appreciation and compassion increases. Your presence is a gift, as you support the open hearts of others also looking for a new way of being.

You are heaven and earth. Your divine expression bridges realities. Love can do no other.

We are in delight with your joy of being.

DAY 176: BUOYED BY APPRECIATION

A resonant match with Love is the being of appreciation. As your days have passed within the matrix of *In Service to Love*, have you noticed an increase in your experience of appreciation?

Appreciation, gratitude, and Love expand equally. As your heart-centered expression of Love expands, so does your appreciation for everything. Situations that used to go unnoticed in their simplicity are now objects of deep appreciation. The look of your Beloved's face as the sun illumines their features, the thrill and magic of nature's sounds previously unnoticed, the flower buds of spring promising exquisite beauty, all now ring with the resonant note of Love. The splendor of the moment is breathtaking when you are no longer engaging in reaction based in the past or the future. Appreciation resides in the Now.

Reaction and living within a restricted viewpoint informed by your past requires a lot of emotional and mental energy, because you are in resistance to your expansive nature. When you are planted within the Now moment the experience of Love, appreciation, and gratitude move to the forefront. There is a breath of release that may be taken as you are no longer expending energy in a whirlwind of concern and managing. When the open space of the Now moment is your nexus, you open to not only possibility but vision only available through your I AM Self.

The presence of Love, gratitude, joy, satisfaction, appreciation, and the profound are all magnified within the Now moment. From the not-Now experience, you are not available to see what lies before you. The not-Now is littered with thoughts, expectations, reactions, and habits; an unaware space occupied with the maelstrom of human living. As you stand in the not-Now, life feels muted and dull. Your unhindered presence in the moment allows the vivid magnificence of truth to be seen and felt. The Now moment is not profound just "sometimes." Now is where profound lives. Profound Love, appreciation, and freedom is your natural way of being.

The experience of contrast is a rich canvas upon which you may express even in the Now moment. As you bring conscious awareness to the process, your moments are unlike any other. The rich pallet of daily experience may be appreciated through the lens of Love.

Your Now moments are the condition that allow you to appreciate deeply. From the window of Now, you see the reality surrounding you newly. The exquisite nature of All becomes clear.

Appreciation is the helium that takes your dreams to the stars. Within the Now moment, being Love and appreciation abounds.

DAY 177: THE TIPPING POINT

You are a force of Love. As the signature energy that is you is turned up, your voice is heard throughout creation. As you bring all of you to the table, you bring also the magnitude of Love, creation, beauty, exquisite compassion, innovation, joy, peace, integrity; all that is uniquely you. There is a tipping point that is reached in your enlightenment process, beyond which the magnitude of light you hold may not be hidden. You are experiencing the naturally expansive nature of your own divine essence.

The tipping point in your expression is a space of no return where the light you hold is the light that becomes your new normal. You shine the brilliance of a million suns in being who you are. The moments spent in the Now are the magnifying force of the expression that is you. There is no way we can describe to you before the fact that the process of enlightenment is the process of you being more of you.

Stepping beyond the tipping point, there is a synchronistic expansion of your light expression. You now hold, integrate, and are stabilized within the space of expansive light. Your ability to sustain the increased capacity you hold for the light that is you is extraordinary, as you express fully the Love you be.

In Service to Love, as a divine collaboration, holds a frequency-rich matrix of light, consciousness, and vitality that evolves. Illumined by Love's grace, we as co-creators, Masters in light, meet you. As your Scribe has declared to Be all that is hers to Be, her willingness to move beyond the known, into the far reaches of her divine expression, quenches the yearning of her soul and the door opens for others. A directive of Love is met. With each strike of the keyboard, the being of *In Service to Love* as a unique, eternal expression of Love is birthed into form.

What else could be possible, beyond the tipping point?

Day 178: More Precious Than Gold

More precious than gold, jewels, and all the riches of the world is the connection to eternal truth you hold.

Love brings with it connection to your expansive divine nature. As you release the barriers to your highest expression, you begin to see the sacred divinity in everyone and everything. Have you not noticed how your judgments and concerns about others have shifted? What you experience within your Self is now reflected in the eyes of all you meet. You hold a natural openness to your being now that was not prevalent before. You have dropped the barriers to experiencing your own greatness. You view your world through the exalted lens of Love. Your encounters are on the phone, in traffic, in your family, at the grocery store, walking down the sidewalk; momentary glances communicate openness, caring, and presence, all reflecting the Love you emanate.

The opening of your connection with All through the lens of Love is a gift beyond compare. How can one even begin to quantify, as Darlene experienced yesterday, the gaze of a small child, inquiring, "Do you know Jesus?" to which your Scribe replied, "Yes, I do." The young girl returned, "Oh, I just know his name." Sweet encounters unfiltered, before barriers are created, exuding Love, light, and connection. The young girl mirrored the openness that is naturally the perspective you hold early in your life. Friends with all she meets, there is nothing and no one that is beyond the embrace of Love and delight.

We would ask you to consider the relationship you hold with us as Masters in light, facilitating *In Service to Love*. There is an openness to possibility that is present in your relationship with us. A space of hope that says, "Even if I don't understand all this, there is truth in the words." The space of openness, of faith, of momentary willingness to drop barriers and filters to your environment, is the same space of being to be extended to others. As you reach deeper into the light that you are, you begin to see yet again that we are made of the same stuff. As you begin to engage with others from a space of honoring who they be, you hold open the space of Love for all to step across the threshold into the brilliance of their own light.

The innocence, brilliance, and truth of a young girl asking, "Do you know Jesus?" demonstrates the extension of Love, beyond any expectations and limitations. In her reality, everyone is held in the exalted space of divine expression.

The golden moments of connection are divine nectar and the high road to illumination.

Day 179: I AM Where Love Lives

As you claim the expression of Love that is only yours, you find the increasing potency of your Now moments.

As you declare your own conscious awareness and enlightenment, engage your highest expression, or commit your intention to view your world from a perspective yet unseen, openings for action are created. The deepest yearnings of your soul are heard whether you hold words for them or not. Your essential Self is ever present, honoring and lighting the way. The clarity of your soul's direction will always lead you to Love.

Although there are many paths to the expression of Love, the path you have chosen, because you are reading these words, is an accelerated path to enlightenment chosen for the specific purpose to contribute the light of Love that you are. The experiences garnered along the way are a beneficent contribution to your unique story and expression. With each soulful thought, experience, wondering, prayer, and profound moment of beauty, you move into alignment with your illumined I AM Self.

Your I AM expression is you, in divine union with the All; your unique soul expression fully realized. Your I AM is where Love resides.

The perceived difficulty of the journey of enlightenment gives way to reveal the perfection that has been at the helm from the very beginning.

I AM

We ask you to consider connecting with your I AM presence.

As you sit quietly, ask your I AM to be felt within you. Ask for a feeling, for a connecting thought, color, symbol. Wait, listen, feel.

You may choose an environment in your meditation that is in nature, or music may guide your movement. Whatever sings to your soul. Allow your mind to soften, releasing thoughts that arise. Visualize your I AM Self and allow the signature energy of your divine nature to align within your human expression. Visualize your perfection. Move to your greatest light expression and hold the perspective of your I AM Self. What do you see? Experience your wholeness.

Gather all the light that you are so that you may know you, as you gaze at your reflection.

Be still, and know that I AM God. We see you and hold the mirror before you, so you may behold the being of light that is your I AM. The resonance of knowing is clear. We invite you to your I AM, where Love resides.

DAY 180: CHANGING THE CHANNEL OF YOUR AWARENESS

The journey of expanding awareness is one of intoxicating beauty and discovery. From the viewpoint of your normal day-to-day way of being, the experiences that begin to unfold are beyond explanation. As you reach into the light of your divine nature, your experience will reflect new depth, breadth, and awareness. Your vision reaches beyond what is seen to what is not seen by most. Your conscious awareness is new to fifth-dimensional capacities.

The conscious presence of your vast nature requests a broader perspective. When you have a "profound" experience, such as viewing auras, feeling light and frequency, past-life recall, or seeing angels, what do you do?

Consider the perspective you hold. Your human nature will naturally view the event through the constraints of the physical world. When you really understand that enlightenment is the process of you claiming conscious connection with your divine nature, profound moments that unfold are reflections of your expansive truth. Enlightenment is the process of wholeness. Change the channel of your perspective.

Change the channel from only hearing the voice of your humanity to include the magnificence, clarity, and gifts of your divine nature as an expression of your wholeness. Listen for your broadest awareness and you will find what has always been so of you. Can you feel your internal dynamic shift?

As you reach deeply into your innate awareness, you move on purpose beyond the constraints of a limited expression. Like the channels on a television, you have many capacities to choose from. An artist's brush is perfect for detail, a paint sprayer covers a lot of ground. You can choose which frame of reference you access. You are All.

We remain,

In Service to Love.

Day 181: Where Is Home?

A sense of home allows your soul to settle. The sacred space of home resides within you. In the material world home has a meaning of family, a structure, a place where you live. For many, the traditional construct of home is not a safe harbor. Home as a space where you feel belonging, acceptance, Love, where you feel seen and find compassion and encouragement is an idealized experience for many on the planet. Beyond the material experience of time and space there exists a home that is inviolate.

When you experience connection with your divine essence, you are home. In your wholeness, the light of your divine nature informs your material life, offering a perspective that is beyond circumstance and appearance.

The purpose of today's conversation is to provide a thought for consideration. What is home for you? Consider that the affirmation of safety, freedom, clarity, connection, and more are available within you each moment. Amid the chaos of transformation around you, the whirlwind of politics, technology, global concerns, and personal transitions, we remind you that the home you seek, the safety you seek, is not found beyond your Self.

Intend your own wholeness, the integration of your divine nature with your human nature. When your environment locally or globally does not hold the security you seek, look more deeply toward your highest expression. In the stillness of your alignment with your divine essence you are home. As you bring the light you are to the forefront, you contribute Love as a healing salve for All.

DAY 182: WHAT WOULD LOVE DO?

L ove, as a creative force, requests a consideration. You are living in a time of deep transformation. The challenge, as with a boat at sea during a storm, is to maintain your balance, clarity, and direction. The maelstrom of information, reaction, opposition, and opinion is a daily onslaught. When faced with challenge, what do you do?

The invitation of Love is ever present. The time of turmoil on the planet Earth activates the inner call for your authentic nature to move to the forefront. It is clear the old ways are no longer working. The new is not yet revealed with clarity. How do you be, as you make the transition from old to new? In times of need, where your new way is not yet formed, you may ask, "What would Love do?" and know in the asking that Love is present.

When events are coming at you quickly, it seems there is nothing available but reaction. This is a normal human experience. When you utilize the words "What would Love do?" Love's presence is ushered in.

What Would Love Do?

So how does one show up in a new way, in moments of crisis or inner inquiry? When you feel reaction beginning to move within you, we ask you to say aloud or to yourself, "What would Love do?" These words create an instant opening and will disconnect your reaction as light shines on a higher-frequency possibility.

One of the hallmarks of transformation is the stage represented by residing within the dark space of the chrysalis. If you look back at your life you will identify other times that are earmarked with the inward focus of transformation. This is a time when clarity seems elusive. It is a time when the old way is no longer working, and the new way is not yet clear. The phrase "What would Love do?" creates an instant connection to your essential knowing that bypasses the experience of "stalling" in reaction or habit. The resonance of these words will call forth your own divine essence. The frequency of these words activates an opening that allows the revelation and peace only available within Love's embrace.

DAY 183: LOVE'S APPRECIATION

Your potent stance aligned with Love accesses your greatest expression. As you ask, "What would Love do?" you move
beyond barriers perceived as impenetrable and you have access to
the divine action and knowing that is your birthright.

From the perspective of right-wrong, good-bad, and the oppositional stance of separation consciousness, Love's presence is not a
tool to manage, control, or persuade. When you hold the intention
for your own wholeness, Love is naturally who you are. Love is your
authentic nature. Love arrives beyond barriers.

Our original intention for our collaboration is in support of
access to all aspects of your divine expression. As you live from the
perspective of aligning with your divine nature, your contribution
of Love transforms and contributes the light of your being across
all creation.

There are three components of this process:

1. REALIZE your expansive divine nature as your authentic
   expression.
2. ACCESS the expansive portion of your being that resides in
   light.
3. UTILIZE the wisdom of your divine nature. This is the purpose of our divine collaboration: the full integration of your
   divine nature with your human nature in a way that makes a
   difference in your life now.

So, when we ask you to move to the space of "What would Love do?" realize it is a quick access to your wisdom and knowing that resides in light.

The appreciation for your willingness to look beyond the perceived barriers of your material reality is lauded. Today, you are gifted with the infusions of Love and light for the appreciation of you. As you receive the infusions of exquisite light, your well-being is supported, ripples of difficulty are eased, and the resonance of peace may be present.

And so it is.

Day 184: Every Day Is a Lucky Day

Good evening, Beloveds. It is I, Thoth, moving to the forefront of this divine conversation within this Now immaculate moment. As your Scribe translates these words, she is (and you are) held in a nurturing state of the maternal principle. Not because something is wrong, but because everything is lined up perfectly. The realization today is that the assurance needed and appreciated is not only received in form, it may be received in light. This is an experience of internal nurturing, healing, and compassion.

As one delves deeper into the light expression that they are, perspectives shift. Today's awareness by your Scribe was a revelation of a new perspective. She feels much is on her plate and is experiencing overwhelm. There has been a sense of isolation in circumstance and recently she has missed the external connection and caring of friends and family conversations. We, as Masters in light, have been the source for most of her conversation of late.

As a part of the transformation in living the reality of an expanding awareness she has been feeling the release of the way of being of the past. New ways of being are opening. Today's revelation is that the connection, assurance, friendship, and caring she receives from friends is also available in light. Not as a replacement, but as the Source of Love.

The hierarchy of support comes first from the Love that is available internally, delivered to the experience in form. Then, the gifts that are naturally available may be gifted, experienced, and expressed into the world. The thought that all that is needed is provided in light first is a new one to grasp. "Why wouldn't I be looking for matters of form to meet needs of form?" Who you are is larger than form.

The old pattern would have Darlene looking for her needs to be met from friends and those close to her. The process of isolation related to current circumstances is temporary and valuable in the message. When she looks to the realm of light and Love for her support, she finds it is not conditional, but is perpetually available and healing beyond description. We are not saying that this is the sole support that is available. Consider, though, that everything you need is given and available within the realm of Love that is your natural expression. The balm of Love is ever present.

Today, Darlene realized the new order of connection. Receive light and Love from the Source of All. Be sustained by the experience. Then, fully aligned with Love, her I AM Self informs, directs, enlightens, clarifies, brings peace, joy, freedom, innovation, and inspiration; in short, All that is her highest authentic expression becomes available. Clearly, this principle applies to you. Love lies within.

The old model would be: Look for support, Love, compassion, and healing within your relationships. Yes, the bonds of Love are extraordinary. However, when they are bound by the limitations and restrictions of the material realm, you run into the constraints of human nature. As you look externally to have your needs met, often expectations are unmet. As you look within, everything you seek is available.

Today has been a potent day of awareness. As Darlene was connected with her Now moments, she was operating on impulse. Impulse originating from internal connection available within the immaculate Now moment. The day was magical in the way the events unfolded. Perfectly in alignment, beyond anything she could plan. Today has been a demonstration of the potency held in light. Not normally a place you would look, we suggest you consider newly.

The potency you hold in your light expression asks alignment of your being with your eternal nature in order to access what is naturally available. Synchronicities, profound moments, gifts, beauty, and Love are all found within the magic of your highest expression. In one of those moments today, a woman said to your Scribe, "Must be your Lucky day!" to which Darlene replied, "Every day is a lucky day."

Begin to look to your inner connection to have emotional needs and concerns quelled. Be curious about the wisdom that you hold naturally. As you look to your divine expression for nurturing, manna, Love, information, compassion, comfort, you find all that and more. As you access the divine expression you are, you become integrated in light. Then, rather than looking for gifts from others to meet emotional needs, you become the contribution you are to All through your being.

The calming of your soul is available in every moment. That is what Love does.

DAY 185: DOORS OPENING TO A NEW REALITY

As you move forward into the expansive nature of your authentic expression, reality shifts as do your perspectives. The unique quality of *In Service to Love* is the component of experiencing the process of enlightenment as your increasing frequency must affect your daily living. Rather than holding actualization as a space that is ethereal and seemingly unreachable from where you stand within your life, our conversations address issues that occur within your day, adjusting your reference of reality. As you take on more of your divine nature as part of you, your realities shift as your awareness expands. Your awareness shifted from kindergarten to college and beyond. There is no staying the same when your awareness expands. We would make a caveat at this point. There is nothing about our conversations that should be implying a movement by you beyond your comfort or beyond your resonant acceptance. There may be stages within the process of *In Service to Love* where you feel complete. We encourage you to follow your own timing and follow your own resonance above all else. You may also choose to do work and then put it down for a while to be picked up again later. It is a lot to grasp within one year. This is a Masters course. Follow your own divine guidance in all matters. This work challenges your known way of being while at the same time answering the deepest yearnings of your soul. You truly bridge worlds. Crossing the bridge, becoming adept at any stage of your vast expression, requires something.

Those present in light buoy your process, supporting you as you choose, allowing ease, clarity, and grace within your discoveries of the many realms of you. Those present include Jeshua, Infinite Oneness, Sanat Kumara, Mary Magdalene, Isis, Melchizadek, Archangel Gabriel, and Archangel Michael.

The caterpillar undergoing the transformative process within the chrysalis reflects what is possible within your own experience. The transformation that is available is complete as the barriers to your divine expression are identified, and bit by bit or in the blink of an eye they are released, revealing the most potent divine expression of you.

As you engage the question, "What would Love do?" you catalyze the internal wisdom you have always held. As you are urged on with stirrings of "the time is now" and your choice for no barriers to your knowing, new realms open before you. What we speak of today is the reality of those realms. The work we do together is real life, your life. Not an idealized expression reaching for the impossible, dependent on a life of hardship. You have in fact already undergone those hardships. Many past lives have been spent with no inkling of the potential held within you.

The possibility exists to align with your divine nature now. As you become adept at releasing the density of your human nature, the light of your divine nature is integrated into your awareness, where the light of Love you hold shines. Your joy, freedom, and fulfillment is at hand, and the contribution you are is met at the highest levels. New realities open before you. No, this is not a dream.

Day 186: Adapting to a Changing World

The world in which you live is always evolving. The work we do together requires skill in adapting to an ever-changing inner landscape. As you change from one state of awareness to another, your human nature will fight for limitations and living within a world of "known," while your divine nature will beckon you beyond perceived barriers. You hold many access points for integrating the vast realms you reside within and which reside within you. The principles we present are applicable equally for your inner world and the material world.

The natural evolutionary process demands an ability to adjust, to be resilient, and to be tenacious to survive. You are responding to pressures of shifting reality on all levels. On the physical plane those pressures are from your environment and the constant influx of information and demands to keep up. If you live your life from the perspective of being an argument for comfort you knew in the past, you miss the boat. The inner realms also point to a new reality you can't place your arms and understanding around.

The challenges of a shifting landscape require conscious skills. Each new level of awareness asks for an ability to adapt. Your ability to be fluid is valuable. As if you are shifting gears, allow your awareness to no longer depend on the material world you see as the only source of truth. Allow your awareness to expand easily as a natural expression of you. As you develop fluidity, you surf the waves of events, gathering that which is yours to see, do, be, and have with ease. Understand there is no loss of potency in being fluid. You may be connected fully to your physical environment and connect easily with the vast expression you hold in light simultaneously.

At times, the thought of inner work feels daunting when immediate needs demand physical-world attention. We remind you there is no separation. As you work on your inner being, you bring your awareness to the skills needed to have an enriching, satisfying physical life. Equally, the physical-world experiences during your day support all the inner knowing, resonance, and contrast needed for your expansion of awareness.

Today we return to ease and delight in what is possible.

DAY 187: THE TRANSFORMING HEART

The tides of change are upon you as you endeavor to expand your awareness to match the reality you inhabit unconsciously as a part of your true divine nature.

As you move through the stages of expanding awareness, you traverse ground that is vast, beyond your comprehension of it. Navigating the nonmaterial world is beyond your ability to think, and therefore employs a greater sensitivity. This is an experience that at times may feel a bit unsettling as you traverse ground that is new territory. On one hand, you experience the reality of your day-to-day living, and on the other hand, the awareness you hold is no longer contained within the reality you view physically.

As your senses expand, so does your constitutional ability to be present within this new expression. It is as though you are acclimating to a new environment. At first feeling foreign, then with more moments spent in the new atmosphere, you gain the ability to become efficient and adept at the ways of being required for the new expanded environment. Your physical being must alter, in ways that are energetic and subtle for most, to the new expansive expression you hold. This often brings on some physical symptoms of discomfort as the new channels of light are opening. There may be times of exhaustion, of feeling weary; your vision shifts, your senses may feel more acutely aware of your environment. Loud noises may be obtrusive where they were not a consideration in the past. As your senses are finely tuned to match the environments of your expanded awareness, there is an adjustment. Follow your internal guidance around the appropriate actions to be taken when these symptoms occur.

Today is an infusion of light, frequency, and coding that galvanizes your heart to the expansive capabilities lying in wait. Today's support is an activation of abilities, sensitivities, and knowing you have held in waiting until your awareness met a level where this is appropriately unlocked. Available is a sense of integration of the stepped-up abilities you now hold. Rather than experiencing the realms as different, they are now more easily and naturally experienced as different gradients of being.

As you choose, and when appropriate, this activation is held for you within your field to be activated at the right moment for your unique expression.

We hold you in a space of reverence and honor your willingness to move beyond the bounds experienced by most. You are the unicorns of the physical realm, bringing light, expansion, and conscious awareness through your beautiful, exquisite expression of Love.

DAY 188: FINDING YOUR NEW CENTER

Each day you see beyond circumstance to the larger perspective that shows the divine at work in every moment. The space you take up consciously has expanded since our collaboration began. What occurs is the reconnaissance into a new realm, often a slight retreat in reaction, then integration into the new space with your awareness which results in an overall expansion. The way you knew yourself to be has shifted beyond expectation. Your access to the light realms of your divine nature is not easily measured in ways you would have employed previously.

Today we speak of the new center of your being, which has altered since you began this journey consciously. We will begin with an analogy. Imagine a balloon without any air in it. Visualize the space that it encompasses. There is potential for more space to be held when the balloon is filled with air, but for now it is not filled. There are specific qualities of a balloon that is not filled with air. It may be tied up, placed in your pocket, it may lie still upon a table, or be placed between the pages of a book. There are a variety of qualities that a balloon holds when it is not filled to its potential expression. Imagine now the same balloon, filled with helium, much like you, now expanded with the light expression you hold. Like the balloon, you take up more space. The qualities held now are different. The expanse is fulfilling a potential of the design of the balloon, but life as a balloon filled with air or helium is quite different from a deflated balloon that lies flat. You emanate more of the light expression that is uniquely you. You are luminescent now in the ways light moves through your being. The signature energy that you hold has turned up in volume. Your sensing in the physical reality is more acute. You feel deeply. You see beyond the limits of most people. You embrace the broader perspective of your Self as a natural expression. More of you is available. You reach into the multidimensional aspects of your being. You hold your presence and attention within a more powerful perspective that is informed by the Now moment. You are transforming into the higher expression of you.

As you have shifted, your center has as well. Just as the center of a balloon not filled with air must shift as the balloon begins to meet its potential by being filled with air, your center of awareness has changed too. Your operating center has shifted to include a greater degree of distinctions. As a wine has a variety of subtle distinctive qualities as it ages, your center "blooms" as your awareness expands. Your "command central" becomes your I AM presence. Events that used to slip by unnoticed now are seen and appreciated in their distinctive qualities within the moment. It's as simple as breathing in the magic of a hummingbird that you see floating in the air in front of you.

Darlene found herself today trying to remember what life was like before she was aware. The same standards for comparison may not be used. Awareness is something you cannot un-remember. You can choose to use it or not. There necessarily comes the need for a whole new set of distinctions that match the ever-increasing vast nature of perspective. The qualities of the balloon without air are different from those of one that is filled with helium. The new dimension of movement must be accounted for.

Your expansive awareness utilizes a whole new set of distinctions. Your divine expression of I AM is your center, speaking to you within each immaculate Now moment. Shhhh, Beloved—do you hear?

DAY 189: AS YOU CONTRIBUTE TO ALL, ALL CONTRIBUTES TO YOU

You are connected to All. It is easier to consider that you are connected to All and contribute to All than it is to consider the contribution All is for you.

Often the experience of connection with All is momentary. When we say you are All, there is truth in the statement. From our perspective there is no separation. All is Love and you are All. From your perspective, ensconced in the daily experience of physical life, the experience of singleness, of separation from each other, is the normal understanding. There exists a reflexive separation that holds borders and division. Do you see the connection between you and the woman in Uganda who travels five miles just for her daily water? There are the people in your life who hold the same cultural connection and then there are people from across the globe who hold a different perspective, and you are in the category of "other" for them. Being connected to All is often assigned as idealism, not necessarily reality.

In the process of expanding consciousness, you have been finding Love is the language spoken by all creation. Who you are at your essential Self is an expression of Love. So far, we have been looking at the process of expanding awareness from your perspective. What does it take to begin shifting awareness to allow new views to be held? How may vision of reality be seen newly? When we refer to newly, we mean an event or concept that introduces an experience that you have no frame of reference for beyond inner resonance. Moving into the larger, more vast expression of your Self in light requires you to shift beyond your current definitions. There must be at some point a letting go of referencing from the past to see something you have not seen before. This is the type of leap that is required to begin seeing the interconnectedness you have with All.

Today we ask you to consider that your connection with All is so complete that you are affected, albeit on the most subtle of levels, by actions of others across the globe. What perspective do you need to hold in order to see what one does, All do? You are contributed to not only by the seeming contrast and failures in character, but in the triumphant spirit of humanity.

The clear voice you hold for your journey to your truth contributes to the choir of All. The defiant voices across the globe support your expression beyond circumstance. Meeting at the common denominator of humanity, we ask you to consider expanding your awareness to discover the connection with those you don't know. When you find courageous events in the news, know you have emboldened their actions through your willingness to also move beyond and shine brightly under the flag of Love. You in turn are elevated in your efforts to express from your soul's vision by those who have come before and those who hold the same image of Love's triumphant declaration.

DAY 190: THE DAWNING OF A HIGHER EXPRESSION

The state of transformation is one that resonates throughout the planet Earth. The action of "labor" is in motion—a specialized movement bringing about a new expression. The feeling of status quo that seemed to be a standard for "being" in past decades is not only difficult to maintain at this point, it is not supported. This is a time when possibilities defined by the past are not expansive enough to write the future of what is now available. On one hand the consciousness of the planet has expanded, making stark the comparative voices of pain. The divergent tones of being cry with a dissonance only made whole by Love.

As the waves of labor form a natural movement of birthing a new expression, understand that the dissonance you see around you and from deep within Gaia are the moans of birth. All is well. As you honor the space you are within, the space of all beings on the planet may be honored as the most perfect expression of the whole. The alchemical action of this time asks for those who are conscious to gently and lovingly be who you are. The divine expression of your awareness holds light in very clear terms, acting as a supporting grid for global transformation.

Those who observe this birthing from the far reaches of creation are in attendance to welcome the new era of enlightenment. As you hold the clarity of your own path, you facilitate and ease the waves of transformation. Consider that the labor of new expression underway throughout Gaia is a mirror for your unique process as well.

Your internal examining, unease, and cry for the vision of your soul and the gentle union of Love is your labor in motion. Dear Ones, we hold you close with the ease of the divine light of your truth. We hold you in embrace with comfort and the remembrance of all you are and all you may be.

DAY 191: FLUIDITY OF PERSPECTIVE

It is I, Thoth, stepping to the forefront as partner and transducer of the energies available in our communications. As Darlene and I connect, I deliver the light frequencies, consciousness, and codes from contributors in light that are *In Service to Love*. Darlene, as Scribe, translates the light, consciousness, and subtle energies into words that hold the matching frequency and composition as the original intention. Darlene shifts perspective each day we connect. There is no one way we communicate; there is an evolving, expanding practice that is at play, as is your experience of expanding awareness. This is truly a multidimensional process. Trying to understand this from a perspective of human nature alone misses the mark.

The process of expanding awareness is one that requires fluidity and resilience. If you are looking at an ever-expanding moving target such as this, your ability to respond in the present moment is required. Consider that your action may not be planned. Consider the fluidity of your life right now as a strength in adapting to your expanding awareness. Fluidity has not necessarily been integral to your past life experience. The unique qualities of this evolutionary process request conscious awareness to be accessed in the moment. So far, we have been focusing on identifying perspectives that have been hardwired into your human experience. Once the active perspective is identified, then it may be brought into conscious awareness and new choices may be made.

The perspective you hold is a powerful determiner of your experience. Human nature contains an energy that repels experience beyond your perspective and instead finds situations that align within the range of the perspective you already hold. The perspective you hold is a template for what is ultimately seen and experienced. Naturally, human nature looks for the affirmation of a known world. Do you see how living beyond the perception of limitations requires fluidity? As you inquire beyond barriers of your perception, the new perspective is invited into your awareness. You are creating pathways for your divine nature to be active in your life consciously. Your unlimited divine nature challenges the limits of your human nature.

As you invite the unseen into your awareness, you are holding a perspective that is fluid. When you acknowledge that the perspective you hold defines the outcome of your experience, you may move beyond inherent limitations. This is so for all areas of your life.

Abundance is one area that is energetically charged for most. Relative to your perspective on abundance, we ask you to consider becoming fluid. As you develop a fluidity in your perspective, you invite avenues of joy, wealth, peace, and ease into all areas of your life. Your past, your beliefs spoken and unspoken, and the collective consciousness of your culture filter your experience. If you choose to see what you haven't seen before, open the lens of your perspective so more is allowed within your field of vision and experience.

We ask you to consider opening the lens of perspective, allowing more to be seen of your true greatness. As you open to experience that shows you just how vast and perfectly unique you are, you will notice all areas of your life expand. What is revealed is the innate brilliance of your divine design, richness in experience and universes of possibility.

DAY 192: REST AND RECEIVE

As you move in your busy days, the need for rest is great. Rest, as you have known it in the past, seems somewhat less fulfilling and not restorative. You now hold a broader expression in light that accesses a vitality, healing, and rest originating in light. Today we speak of recharging your light stores. Those present in light today accompany you in the process of breathing in newly the rest and relaxation you have been calling for in the realms of light.

Today, as we (your Council of Light) speak, we are on an experience together, if you so choose. Today, in this Now moment, we relax in a boat together, reclining in comfort as we float down the river Nile. There is nothing to do, there is nowhere else to be. We take in the beauty, magnificence, and gift of every sight and sound about us.

On the Nile

As we float comfortably together, in this simple boat of reeds, there is no way of being other than simply being. As Love is recognized as the Source of All, how could we be any less? As the barriers to being are dropped within the high-frequency locale of our meeting, the softness exists of no-thing and every-thing being the space we occupy. You are noticing the beauty of the moment with no agenda other than the magnificence of the experience. Our presence is simply to lead you to the space of no-thing, of immaculate presence in the moment, which allows you to be gifted completely by each fleeting fragrance, the light of the sun as it reflects off the water's surface and through the trees on the river's bank.

This experience is a gift available for you if you choose. As we meet in this high-frequency space of rest, what is occurring is activation of a restorative mode. Sleep supports your physical and general well-being; this is another tool available to you that both accesses and supports your expansive expression.

You bridge realities as you occupy a broader range of the gradient light expression of your being. There is an experience of inefficient use of energy in the process of expansion. So as you are shifting from the reality you have known to the new, vast expression of you that resides in light, you have more resources at your avail. Allow high-frequency experience to contribute to you. There are new ways in which to receive, restore, and recharge from the light that is your essential nature. Rather than addressing solely your physical body's needs, you may expand your perspective to account for the expanded reach you now hold in light.

The energetic demands of this evolutionary process are eased through your awareness of what it takes to support your overall well-being. The benefit of our excursion together is to lead you to another way of being within a high-frequency realm that ultimately contributes to you. You may utilize high-frequency experience such as this to fuel and recharge your expression both in light and form. Your light expression telegraphs information to your physical being. As you expand conscious awareness to include parts of you that reside in light, you are stepping back and taking moments to restore all parts of you through this process. It doesn't need to be a trip down the river Nile; it may also be a vivid, high-frequency experience of your making. It must contain elements of nature that support you, envelop you, and contribute to you. Allow the moments to reflect the magnificence of your true nature back to you, filling your being with the manna you may revel within and be revitalized by.

Look, Beloved: Do you see the heron on the river's bank?

DAY 193: THE COLLECTIVE OF LOVE

G ood evening. It is I, Thoth, accompanied by the voices of many
that move to the forefront of this divine conversation within
this Now immaculate moment. The experience today is very fine in
its vibration, a new subtle range of information that may be heard
through the collective of Love.

In Service to Love is an example of the collective of Love. As the
name implies, Love is the common denominator. The voice of Love
is one that is heard from all corners of creation as the ultimate truth
in expression and at the core of being, generation, and principle.
Today's message is one that holds the intention of connection at a
high frequency that offers an even broader perspective. The vast
perspective allows you to see your unique expression of Love in alliance within the collective of Love. All part of the One, standing for
the expansion of Love, peace, and freedom for All.

The collective of Love is one that is active, with each being
expressing the perfection of their divine design, who then when
joined with others create the harmonic of Love's collective.

As you consciously join in the collective of Love, the message
of your unique expression is joined with many and the difficulties
felt at the point of not-Love are washed by Love's collective action.
As you move farther into the light expression of your authentic
nature, you experience the collective consciousness of Love. If you
choose, your voice may be added to support the efforts of Love,
bringing sustenance of light and Love to those that await the rescue
of Love's light.

The collective of Love contributes in each Now moment, holding Gaia in assuring embrace as the evolutionary process unfolds. Through your intention, your voice may be added. If you are called, there is no-thing to do, only BE the Love that you are.

Love's triumph is the triumph for All. The collective of Love is supported by those beings in light joining forces in their unique expression. You may send the gift of your Love to all corners of creation through your intention as you join the voices of Love's collective action.

DAY 194: ANCIENT DNA

The process of expanding awareness that has you fulfill your high-est expression is foretold in your DNA. The DNA is the stuff that identifies you as you. There are specific and unique earmarks within your DNA that tell your history in form as well as in light. Your full potential is also held in waiting within your DNA light codes.

Your totality of being, your full expression is held as possibility within your DNA light structure. Whether parts are fulfilled within this life or the next are up to you in each immaculate Now moment. For example, the way to best look at the action of your DNA is to understand the thresholds you must pass in order to become an adult. All actions held within your DNA, from infant, toddler, child, adolescent, teenager, to adult, and the expression of you as a being of light in form is also held in your DNA coding. In the same way thresholds are crossed in order to move from one stage of your life to another, so too are there certain thresholds in levels of conscious-ness that open as particular criteria are met within your awareness. One level of conscious awareness will support the access point for the next stage. You hold the DNA light coding for full conscious aware-ness. You truly are not gathering anything beyond your Self, as you explore your divine nature. There is nothing outside of you as you access the expression of you that resides in light. In fact, you are acti-vating consciously those gifts that are already a part of your design.

The total fulfillment of your divine design is a potential that many do not achieve. The process of *In Service to Love* holds the mirror to what is already there within you, so that you may begin to look newly within the vast space of your being.

As you look deeply within, in search of your truth, the expanse that is present may not be overstated. As you gaze into the night sky, through the stars and planets within your vision, look between the glittering veil to see beyond. As Jeshua proclaimed to your Scribe early on, "*All this is inside you.*"

DAY 195: LOOKING INWARD

In the expansion of awareness there are times of uncertainty as new ground is trodden within an ever-changing landscape. It is easy to be disoriented at times as what you know keeps changing. The purpose of our conversation today is to remind you of the brilliance and wisdom that resides within you. We remind you to reference within. You hold wisdom so great it could never be contained within the largest of libraries or the greatest of computers. You are a multidimensional divine expression of Love.

We ask you to consider today to clarify how you attain guidance. Often the questions and prayers are for guidance that is contained within the wealth of information you already hold. It is a moment to reorient yourself again to the expanse that resides within you. When your choices in life are in direct conflict with that which you pray for, it is your intention that speaks. The experience may be one of being disappointed that a request was not honored. Instead, may we point out the request for clarity. The request for clarity allows you to hold a new perspective that contains the resolution or new piece of information that is helpful to move forward. Rather than being given an answer, you hold the dynamic, empowering access to the wisdom you already hold. Consider that you are in an ever-changing process. Within your divine design is the answer to all you may ever need as you connect with the expression of Love that you are.

Often prayer sets up a dynamic that holds you separate from Love, like being outside looking in. As you take on the reality of your own divine nature you see everything you need is already within you as All. This distinction is subtle. For most it does not make any difference. For you, a Master in the process of expanding consciousness, we point you toward that which will make a difference in the process of enlightenment. These are Master-level conversations.

Connect Now

At times when you may feel disconnected from your own genius, we suggest you call all parts of you to be present. Take a deep breath and turn up the signature energy signal that amplifies your expression. There will be a sense of renewal as you claim the light of the knowing that is yours.

> *I bring all parts of me present here and Now.*
> *I bring all parts of me present here and Now.*
> *I bring all parts of me present here and Now.*
> *Take a deep breath.*

Please know we stand beside you and we stand behind you. We honor the brilliance of the divine expression you hold. Through the light of our countenance we reflect to you, your own sacred expression.

DAY 196: CHANGING THE CHANNEL

Your day naturally demands a physical presence. In addition to expanding your conscious awareness, consider that you are expanding in your physical expression as well. There are times when the two realities seem to misalign and the space of ease that exists at the perspective of your expanded Self feels absent. Today we speak of the ease of changing the channel.

When you feel during your day as though your perspective has slipped into a space of dulled routine, you will have red flags in your experience. Your energy will drop; there will typically be a reactionary thought process. There is a sense of overwhelm, a sense of hard work, a sense of being defeated with no solution handy. This is an experience that occurs often as a part of the experience of contrast. It represents habits and patterns from the past; there is usually a line of conversation that is familiar. Overlying the experience is a sense of not being empowered. There is a diminishing of Self that is present within this perspective.

The purpose of our conversation today is to remind you that you have new tools, new consciousness, and new ranges of frequency at your disposal. Not to fix discomfort, but to access your own potency. If you do not like the space you are within, if you are feeling unempowered, if you are feeling exhausted because of the mental and emotional weight you hold, you may make a new choice. In the same way you change the channel of the TV, you may also change the channel for your way of being. In the past, the way of being we are speaking of may have been a default or a regular character in your play. If you don't like where you are, change the channel. It is that simple. You have new tools available. A new remote, so to speak.

Change the Channel

Stop what you are doing when you realize you are feeling disempowered.

"Oh, I am doing that again! This is only one choice. I have many choices."

Become present in the realization. "I bring all parts of me present here and Now. I bring all parts of me present here and Now. I bring all parts of me present here and Now."

Take a deep breath.

Move to the adjustment process you have for amplifying your signature energy. (This could be a communication tower, a volume dial, a light turning on, a big red button.) Amplify your signature energy. Take another three deep breaths. With each breath, breathe in the light that is surrounding you. You stand tall owning all the light expression that is you. You are once again trued up with your divine nature. Your light expression is aligned with your physical presence.

And then, with a new perspective, you move into your day with an empowered perspective. The drag of resistance is gone as you are aligned. You feel lighter, clearer, empowered. You fill up the space that is yours.

This is a beautiful process. As you realize fully the capacity you hold naturally for empowered and conscious action within the moments of your days, you set the trajectory for awareness, events, and synchronicity that further supports the expression of the highest, most expansive part of your being.

The beauty of you may not be hidden. We see you.

DAY 197: YOUR NORTHERN STAR

The northern star was the point of nighttime navigation for early explorers. Always reliable, dependable, a source beyond reproach. You, too, hold the internal direction that is eternal. Those present in light for our conversation today bring the resonance of their being in support of you.

Your northern star shines through the depths of darkness to reveal a path of light. The guidance available for you is ever present, eternal, and is the keystone of your being. Your northern star is your fully realized expression, beyond form's limitations and beyond time and space. Your God Self, all knowing, is connected seamlessly with All and expresses uniquely through you, your I AM presence. If you are quiet enough to hear newly, you will find wisdom, clarity, compassion, freedom, abundance, and Love, as it flows through you naturally. The resonance of your I AM presence is Love of the highest order. Your I AM presence, like the northern star, holds a vision and perspective that is far beyond what may be seen with the physical senses. As you finely tune your high-frequency awareness, you find resonance with your divine nature.

At this point in *In Service to Love*, we shift focus to your I AM presence. Developing communication and identification with your highest divine expression is the opportunity at hand. For each of you, reading these words, as you choose, your I AM presence shall shine more brightly for you, creating an opening for a deeper awareness, connection, and communication. When we say there is nothing you don't already know or that you already have all you need, the Source of that expression is your I AM.

Your I AM presence stands in perfect alignment as pure Love, being. There is an infusion of light that is available today if you choose that catalyzes awareness at a new level.

One quality of the northern star is its placement in the sky, unreachable yet ever present. Your I Am Self holds the highest perspective of Love and therefore is an eternal beacon for your direction, choices, and knowing.

The Path of Light

Relax, and release yourself into the light of Love, divine knowing, and the sacredness of your being. Allow Love's divine light to inform you, igniting your essential expression. The path of the I AM is expansion. As you expand in your process of enlightenment, there is territory you also leave behind. Not that it is gone, but that new choices are being made that propel you ever beyond.

This is not a journey of inertia; it is a journey of expansion and moving forward, beckoned gently yet persistently by your I AM presence.

We hold you in the light of Love. We remain In Service to Love.

DAY 198: ADJUSTING TO 5D ACCESS

The ascension process is all about bringing that part of you that resides in the space of light into your physical experience beyond the boundaries and limitations that are inherent within the physical 3D world. As you begin to live from the knowing and the high-frequency perspectives that are available within your divine expression, your experience within the physical world is altered. You become untethered by the weight of issues that would stop you or become barriers to your expression. Today, there is new access to the experience of you that resides in light.

There is a new way of being that is available to you in relation to your physical experience. You hold the ability to access your 5D knowing as a new way of being. Consider that the 3D way of being is the understanding of most. For those yearning for the more that is available, you sense the limitations of the 3D experience as your multidimensional Self requests expression. The best way to look at the difference is by noticing how you look at your physical experience. Within a 3D perspective, what you see is understood as the totality of reality: "I believe because I see it." In 5D reality, what you see is an effect of something else. The vast perspective of your divine nature sees beyond limitations of physical reality. In 5D experience you hold a distant perspective that allows you to see the perfection of each moment.

In 5D reality, you conduct your physical expression from the knowing you are All. Your experience is driven by your soul's vision rather than the events of your day. You create consciously from a space of empowerment. As you see the divine expression of your essential Self, that becomes an active component in your moments. You begin to listen rather than hear, you hold vision rather than see. You emanate the light you are and bring the resonance of truth to your presence.

We are nearing two-thirds of the way through the year and a day of *In Service to Love*. The reach you hold into the light of your divine expression is considerable. You notice a new way of being in the physical world that accommodates your new expression. It is at times not comfortable as you unplug from one way of being to allow a greater expression to be manifest. It is at that tipping point of expression where the 3D way of being is in the rearview mirror and the 5D way of being is not yet fully understood, that you will notice you may feel like a "fish out of water." This is temporary. Consider that you are creating a larger home or energetic grid to support the greater expression of you that is in light. Your Scribe has been experiencing a sense of completion, a sense of loneliness, not related to connection with anyone else but intrinsic to her being at this time. That is due to a new connection that is developing. Although in light, manifestation is quick, when the signal moves through the density of form there is a time frame to contend with. This is part of the process.

The butterfly within the cocoon has a specific process of transformation, as do you. There is an ebb and flow of experience as you expand your conscious awareness. The process of reaching into the light expression you are is your process of in-lightenment. It is a different way of being that encompasses everything you know and includes so much more of your divine expression, empowerment, joy, well-being, creative expression, and abundance on all levels. The connection for seamless communication between your divine nature and human nature is a part of the natural process of expanding awareness.

This is not necessarily a black-and-white process. Your expansion involves many layers of your being only made available once they become unburdened by the weight of limitations of the 3D perspective. Follow your own guidance in all matters, being responsible for your well-being and care.

Allow the new view of your Self to surprise and delight you. You are supported in every step with the sacredness of being.

DAY 199: YOUR EXPANDED PERSPECTIVE

As your awareness expands, you hold a new perspective. Adjusting to the influx of information that is now available is a part of your journey of enlightenment. Utilizing the information accesses a new facet of your expression.

The cohesion of your energetic field holds you in alignment at your highest expression. Over the past few days we have discussed ways in which to address the feeling of misalignment or wobble in your experience. Now that you have increased access to your knowing in light, there is a light, or energetic field, to be conscious of. When you feel out of alignment, rather than choosing a new way of being, look first toward the aligning of your fields. Is there an integration of your light that is being requested? Do you require an amplification of your signature energy?

Once you feel aligned, like the unkinking of the garden hose, you are available for optimal access of your highest knowing. As your Scribe sits with us daily, development of a daily practice is a source of support for the deepest connection available. The most profound of gifts are waiting within. The old ways of habit and reflex are diminishing, and the conscious connection with your inner voice is paramount. As the artist must sit before the canvas, and the musician must practice their instrument, you, as the creator of your life, must meet the silence and allow the inner voice of your soul to be heard.

Your divine nature informs your physical experience adding perspective and dimension. This is where inner work is inescapable. Informed by your I AM Self, your access to fine frequency becomes integral in your physical life. To progress along the avenue of expanding consciousness, the expanding consciousness must be utilized. Like the finest of sports cars, potential is accessed through action. The car must be placed into gear first. Otherwise potential remains in the garage. There is a point where you may choose to have your physical life as you know it contributed to by your inner knowing, and life will be experienced with more ease, joy, and freedom for sure. The next moment requires another choice. And be clear: The choice is only yours. If you choose to manifest your soul's vision, you must be connecting with the voice of your soul. *In Service to Love* is designed specifically for the expansion of conscious awareness, the realization and actualization of your soul's voice as your divine expression.

The path of enlightenment is a contribution to your life's experience bringing joy, empowerment, freedom, wisdom, ease, and connection that is authentically you. And there is always more. Another space of light has opened. The next step requires your specific choice to connect with your inner voice.

Allow the silence to give voice to your I AM.

You are in the most unique of positions, joining worlds. That is how vast you are.

DAY 200: CELEBRATION; BASKING IN THE LIGHT OF LOVE

The magnificence of the divine expression of Love that you are is breathtakingly beautiful. Do you understand you need do nothing to be perfect? Do you see that the expansion of your conscious awareness is purely by choice, not a mission, not a job, not needed? Who you are as you are in this Now moment is perfection. It is easy, within the looking for the "more" that is possible, to miss the perfection of the moment. We bring attention today back to the Now moment of beauty and Love's grace.

Today is about the celebration of your divine expression. It is easy to move to the category of hard work when one chooses expansion of consciousness. There is a hypersensitivity that is developed in looking beyond the appearance of what lies before you. Your ability to sense is heightened; you are gathering more information than you know what to do with at this point. The light of your being shines brilliantly. The radiance of your being emanates Love's warmth and healing balm. As you gather more of the light unto you that is your authentic expression, your presence transforms.

There is no in-order-to here. When we say expansion of consciousness is a choice, it is true. You don't need to do anything or be anything beyond your exquisite Self to be held in the adoring embrace of Love. If you strip away the inner drive to find more, if you strip away the straining to hear the voice of your soul, if you move beyond the willingness to no longer be constrained, there is You. You at your most essential Self, right here, right now, moving through your day.

It is true; the contribution you are to Love's voice is extraordinary. You tread a path not commonly chosen. You move through the discomfort of the known to birth the sacred unknown. You are seen. You are heard. You are held on high.

Today you are offered an infusion of light, gifting the ease, grace, and joy of appreciation for your exquisite being. Breathe in the light and bubbles of exhilaration. All for you.

Today you are celebrated. You are celebrated for the sheer beauty of you.

Day 201: Stepping into Light
with Ease

As your awareness moves deeper into the expression of light that you are, there are times when words no longer engage you at the most beneficial level. Today is one such day. The movement into light has been extraordinary. There has been a realigning of your physical expression with your divine nature, bringing parts of you together to create a cohesive experience that sets you on a solid base for future movement. As we move into new and more expansive territory, you feel subtle shifts in the cadence of our communications. This is in part led by the intentional flow of the Council members through the intention for each day's conversation.

Today is a day of adjustment in light. There is celebration for the divine expression of you, as you are, here in this Now moment. Those stepping to the forefront of this divine conversation so we may speak with a unified voice of Love is Jeshua, Mary Magdalene, Infinite Oneness, Isis, Melchizadek, Metatron, Archangel Michael, Archangel Gabriel, Sanat Kumara, the Dragons of Love, Legions of Light, St. Germain, St. Francis.

The topic today is the space of ease that is available as you integrate more of the light expression that is you. The message will be relayed via light and frequency. There is nothing to do, other than sit, relax, and breathe in light. The emanations of the Council of Light provide an enriching component that through your own timing connects and prepares you for the movement that is to come. Manifestation occurs first in light, then shifts into the levels of form. So we prepare for our next steps from the light of Love first.

There is a time where between your inhale and your exhale, you contain the All. This is where we are at this moment.

It is with a gentle embrace of Love's assurance that we bid you sweet dreams. Rest easy knowing you are held in Love.

Day 202: Utilizing Your Expanded Awareness

There are new faculties that are gained through your expanded awareness. Your being now plays new notes. Rich harmonics are available for you within your day. Those present today in light bring their own brilliance to support your acclimation to the qualities that are innately yours.

The expanded space you find yourself within is familiar, resonant, and yet distinct from the way your days have been going previously. Within a familiar environment you somehow feel different, not relating to your surroundings in the way you have in the past. The shift you are experiencing reflects the expanded awareness that you have access to. Your environment is viewed through a new vision. It is when you align your vision with your knowing that a new perspective may be attained.

It is not as though the new awareness you hold will solve all your perceived problems, and it would be an error in thinking to assume this is so. What now becomes available is the new perspective. When you step back from an issue or event what becomes available is the additional information only accessed through a new view of the issue. When you hold a strong to opinion or thought about something, you are locked into that viewpoint and other possibilities are not accessible even though they exist within the All there is. This new perspective offers a broader view that takes into consideration possibility beyond the experience of judgment and belief. Judgment and belief are recognized for their limitations in the moment, offering an opportunity for choice. Within the enlightenment process you access a direct aligning with your divine nature that is not informed by the limitations of judgment and belief systems of your human nature.

The shift in viewpoint may be likened to standing on sand and looking only at your feet. With a new perspective you lift your head and see a broader landscape that provides context. Beyond the sand at your feet lies the horizon, beach, the ocean waves, the light shining on the water's surface and the vista in the distance. Your expanded awareness provides you access to a new view.

At times there may be a slight disorientation as you seem to reevaluate everything you thought you knew. This is the aligning process that has been underway over the past few weeks. Do you see that as you begin to fill the space that you already own, your stability in perspective is supported? The attachment to day-to-day events is somehow a bit more distant as they no longer hold the energetic meaning they did before.

Connecting with your expansive divine nature in and of itself provides the calm seas you look for. Understanding the reason for the possible reorienting is valuable information.

The shift in perspective in the process of aligning with an expanded consciousness transitions you from defining your life according to what you have known in the past to what you feel and sense in the moment. Resonance is the new method of connection with your highest expression.

This may sound simple, but when you have a lifetime of relating to your world in one way and another way opens, the reality may feel disorienting. That is why this is a choice point. We have communicated that you are at choice in each moment. You may not feel that shifting your reality to that extent is for you, and that is an empowered choice.

Reorienting to an Empowered Perspective

When you find yourself a bit disoriented, ask, "What else is there for me to see here? I choose clarity in this moment." Give yourself some time to process the new information. Rather than coming quickly, as do your beliefs, the new empowered perspective will arise from your inner knowing. The experience will be a bit slower than your thinking, as your resonant system is more finely tuned. Allow the communication to rise to meet your awareness. Be curious about how you receive information from your highest perspective. Trust your own process. You are a Master.

Adjusting to a new perspective is a skill. Consider the freedom you hold as your I AM Self is offered full expression.

Day 203: New Neural Pathways

When you reach for new aspects of your divine expression consciously, your whole being adapts in accommodation. Today we speak of the brilliant adaptive patterns you possess.

The brilliance of the divine design is at play as you expand your capacity of consciousness. The adapting, aligning, and integrative properties we have been speaking about throughout the development of *In Service to Love* all point to the fact that your highest divine expression is meant to be attained. The qualities of enlightenment are not just held out for those that deem themselves to have gone through Love's "threshing floor" as Rumi called Love's trials. The trials are those that are inherent within the human experience as normally held constraints. You are designed for full expression of your divine nature available in your life now.

Many of the ways of being you have held thus far in your life were determined by you before you entered this lifetime. They have been supported by the beliefs, experiences, and expectations of your frame of reference. Your external reality then responds accordingly, having your reality around you fit within the bounds of your expectations. When you decide to expand your awareness and take on the light that is your divine nature, your being responds to the force of your intention, opening new realities and therefore calling into question the beliefs, judgments and definition of experiences you had held as defining keystones of your human experience. The act of inquiry and reevaluation from a larger perspective reveals possibilities never entertained previously. New choices open the doors for potential to be realized.

The message to be conveyed today is of your natural ability to adapt to the expanded perspective you bring to your day's moments. As you reach thresholds of understanding that are in resonant alignment with your highest expression, you begin to adapt, opening new neural pathways to accommodate your persistent exploration into the arena of what is possible. Your brain begins to rewire to accommodate the new requests. In many other times of your life, your body will adapt as you meet specific thresholds. You also adapt, calling into action those qualities that have been dormant; in this case, your capacity for actualization of your divine nature. Many do not look past the perceived solidity of their physical reality, so the need for adapting to a larger, more expansive way of being lies in potential.

You already hold everything you need for your enlightenment. As you open doors to an ever-expanding reality, your being resonates with the truth. Love's light beckons you forth as, one by one, the new facets of your being are unveiled.

DAY 204: THE BELLS TOLL
FOR YOU

Those moments you spend idly entertaining possibility, your so called "daydreaming," is valuable beyond measure. It is the action of your divine knowing in connection with your physical expression. In those moments you are in open communication involving the All of your being. It is this activity we speak of today. Today, the bells toll for you.

When you watch flocks of birds crossing your evening sky, you will notice there are usually a few of the flock that are the leaders. They support the well-being of the whole flock by flying in a key position of leadership. There is no extra thought process that has them assume that role. They are fulfilling the unique qualities of their design. You, too, are a leader of the flock. The inner yearning that is at the core of your being is not the active quality for most. What is it that makes leaders different? Leaders of enlightenment move beyond the mastery of life to direct their attention to the mastery of being. You, as a leader of thought, seek the wisdom of your divinity. When others are looking outside for direction, you look inward and beyond consensus.

It is in those moments of engagement with idle moments of contemplation, lost in the magnificence of the moment, when you begin to hear the calling of your being. The exalted moments of connection with your very essence brings meaning, depth, and possibility to your days. This is a gift of the greatest magnitude. There is no greater gift than you.

We encourage you to continue the act of "mental doodling," engaging the space of no-thing that in turn holds All. When you move beyond the walls formed by perceived constraints you see the way through. You see the brilliance of the whole picture. As you entertain what could be around the next corner, you create beyond limitations. You forge new space with your "What if?"

The intention to move "beyond," to live the reality of the highest expression, is the act of a visionary. You hold open the space of possibility. You hold the light of hope, assurance, and faith that the dream of the I AM is a reality. You tread new ground and reflect the light of "the new world" elevated by Love.

You are held in the arms of Love and in appreciation of your pursuit of divine expression.

The bells of the cathedral of the sacred toll for you.

DAY 205: THE TONIC OF MEDITATION

As Darlene and I connect, there is a subtle energetic stream of consciousness that joins us. If you would, imagine a spoonful of honey that is being held high above a cup of tea. Due to the consistency of the honey, there are times when the honey is on the spoon, above the teacup, and in the teacup at the same time. The connection we hold spans realms of light and frequency. The transferring consciousness is delivered to your Scribe. As I, Thoth, transduce the message, Darlene again transduces the frequency and translates the message. There is much to learn within the process of connection where, from the perspective of divine collaboration, you place yourself in the position of being able to listen. What is there, waiting, for you to receive? Those present today are many as they are in wait for the connection with you at the next level, a level that better lines up with the space in light you can hold. Your divine team unique to you are present today.

As you move through your day's moments, being in the material world holds requirements. You shower, sleep, eat, exercise, work, play, clean your home. All these activities contribute to the quality of your day and they are activities that are appropriate for the human experience. As you extend your awareness into the light expression of your being, there are other activities that contribute to the quality of your experience. Today we speak of meditation as a multipurpose tool for your well-being on all levels.

As you meditate, your brain waves shift from being alert to deeper awareness and states of relaxation. As you release awareness of your external surroundings, you see within. Much may occur as you move into the depths of your own inner universe. There are two modalities attained through meditation that we speak of today: restoration through relaxation and restoration available through connection.

Relaxation

As you sit still, breathe deeply. Visualize and feel stress and tension as it flows from your body. Focus on releasing tension held at your feet, ankles, calves, thighs, into your hips, abdomen, stomach, chest, back, shoulders, arms, and neck, and move awareness to your face and the top of your head. Feel the release as tension no longer supports you. Your breathing calms, your breathing is gentle, as you move into a deeper state of awareness. You hold the ability to sense more keenly. Your breath slows down.

From this deep space, hold the intention for relaxation and allow the relaxing to restore all parts of you. You may visualize an environment that is comforting, a memory, a space that supports your ability to release all burdens and be present in the sea of Love. Allow yourself to be wrapped with a ceremonial blanket, holding you and cherishing everything about you. Release, relax, and restore.

Connection

From the space of deep relaxation, shift your intention to connection. The experience of connection is uniquely yours. We suggest, for the purpose of this meditation, allow yourself to feel and register the energetic field you are within and the field of frequency you connect with. Allow yourself to sense newly. As you connect with your I AM Self, you align your human nature with your divine nature. Feel the expansive space of awareness.

As you relax, breathe deeply, releasing tension with each breath. As you approach stillness declare your intention to raise your frequency. "I raise my frequency Now." Feel the shift. As if stepping up into a new realm, feel an open, lighter space. Consider that the open space is also a field of frequency. Within the vast field of no-thing, further fine-tune your awareness to see the rich field of potential. Fine-tune your awareness to focus on what is present, not what is absent. The thoughts, words, and feelings of this space are not your imagination. Trust your intention for connection. You are also entraining to a higher frequency in aligning with your divine nature.

Meditation, whether for relaxation or connection, is subtle. As you experience more time in meditation you are setting up the safe harbor of your connection with you as a being of light and with your divine team, guides, and guardians. Your team will feel very familiar, safe, and known. When you turn your attention inward you release the external specifics and gather information from the parts of you beyond form. Your access to your inner world holds clarity. You will find the inner connections are always restorative. Allow yourself to be restored by the experience. You will recognize the energetic fields of the team that surrounds you so lovingly. Each connection with your divine team is also deeply restorative.

Creating the time to honor the being of you that resides in light allows a venue for you to speak to you. How may your soul be heard if you are not in the room? Developing your skill for connecting with your I AM Self and the realms of Masters in light allows opportunity for divine collaboration.

Engage Love.

Day 206: Creating, Positioning, Timing

Today we speak of the methodology at the core of the rhythms of your life.

Consider that the methodology or structure of "how life goes" has been run by your automatic system of default messaging. Now, with your expanding awareness, the old structure is not sufficient to hold the potential of you. Now the structure at the core of your day's events shifts as your conscious awareness expands. As you take on more of the light knowing of you, your inner seasons or natural timing becomes apparent. For example, your Scribe and her Beloved were in the market for a new home. They did a lot of shopping. She found a home that resonated deeply, and she declared, "I want that home." However, the home she wanted was not for sale. Three months later, it went on the market. They now live in the home that resonated at first sight. A perfect fit, at the perfect time. When you align with your highest expression, you set into motion a series of events that answers your request.

As you step on board the ship of expanding awareness, one thing you can count on is movement. The skill of steering an ever-shifting perspective is paramount within the process of enlightenment. The fluidity of being is what keeps you moving within the process. When you hold a perspective that says you create everything, from the ego-centric expression of your mind, you are limited to utilizing only that part of your expression and the limitations held around time and creating. The mind can wield tremendous creations. However, when you shift your perspective to include the wisdom that is available through your I AM Self, your highest expression, the doors open wide to creations that are a match for your soul's authentic nature Now.

When your creations draw upon your nonlinear divine nature, resonance accesses possibility beyond the limitations held by your human nature. Resonance is what occurs when what you are thinking or choosing is in alignment with your highest Self. If you are wanting to create something and there is no resonance present, it will not occur. Or if it does, the frequency of the creation will not ring and the creation will be informed by unconscious constraints. The frequency of the creation will have a thud or flat feeling to it.

When your way of being is informed by your soul's voice you reach into the vast field of potential that is you. This is key. There is a distinction to be made around the source of your decisions and creations. If they come from the vast space of your expanded Self, then you have access to everything that lies within that field. If your way of being is held within the constraints of what your mind thinks is possible, your creations are equally constrained. This points to your creations being a frequency match for you.

As you spend more time aligning with your highest expression, you will see there is a "positioning" that occurs. As you hold the intention of creating based upon resonance sourced from your divine nature, what you will find is circumstances and opportunity that are beyond what you could have thought up. Divine timing is the mechanism of your highest expression moving heaven and earth to bring that which resonates with you at the highest levels into your physical reality. When you begin to see there is not a linear connection with what you choose to create, you are open to receive from all avenues of your life.

You are gifted with events from your highest expression daily; a hummingbird, a butterfly, a rainbow just for you, a song that relays words that calm your soul, and since your soul does not distinguish small or large, your heart's vision may come into view. Open your perspective yet wider to see the communications from you to you and see the masterful chess game of positioning that is occurring.

Day 207: Beyond All Else

When your days are challenging, when you are feeling in struggle, when you are not feeling well, beyond all else, there is Love. Those present today bring blessings of Love, support, and resonance of your truth.

When you live within an era of transition such as the time now, the experience on many levels feels as though you have set sail on the high seas unprepared. We may support you with ideas, strategies, light infusions, and guidance, but when it gets down to it, *you* are living the magic of your days.

There are choices made every moment during the days, weeks, and months of your life. It is easy to move to a default position as a space of habit and respite. Today we remind you to engage Love.

If you do not have an answer, if you are confused, if you are not feeling well, beyond all else, there is Love. As you make choices that engage Love you are always moving in the right direction.

When you engage Love, you call upon the highest expression possible. The act of calling upon Love acknowledges that the universe conspires to your benefit.

Beyond all else, there is Love.

Engage Love.

DAY 208: CHERISHED BY LOVE

As spring's warm gentle rain nourishes and restores the plants hardened by winter's cold, so does Love's eternal embrace restore the wells of your being.

The Love you bestow upon yourself is the topic of our conversation. One of the basic principles of *In Service to Love* is that YOU are Source in form. Who you are at your very essential Self is Love's reflection. Those present in light today remind you of the boundless quality of Love.

Your potential is expansive as you align your presence in form with your presence in light. As you access the light that is your natural expression, you resonate beyond the limitations of form. You get in step with your authentic expression. You resonate Love. Your unique characteristics become the expressions of Love in its many facets.

As you move through your life experiencing the contrast and brilliance that is yours, there is a fundamental action of giving more than you receive. Today we remind you of the boundless, eternal quality of Love that you are. As you stand in the eternal fountain of Love, allow Love to restore your being. Drink in Love's gifts. Receive the Love that is yours. As you do, you align more with your natural expression. As you are aligned, your experiences align, your thoughts align, your presence emanates truth.

Who you are is the divine expression of Love. Feel the Love as it brings life to every cell of your very being. It is easy to express your Love through compassion and support of others. Consider the eternal font of Love that is available for you. Remember to allow the Love that surrounds and moves through you to restore, inform, and generate your moments.

Bask in the Love that you are.

Embrace Love as you are embraced.

DAY 209: THE DIVINE PRINCIPLE
OF ONE

The elevated state of Oneness is the topic of our conversation today. It is I, Thoth, stepping to the forefront of this conversation that may not occur in anything other than this magnificent Now moment. Those present in light supporting the process of remembering enlightenment include Jeshua, Mary Magdalene, Infinite Oneness, the Collective of Love, Abraham, Isis, Melchizadek, the Legions of Light, the Hathors, and Golden Stargate.

Within this process of enlightenment that is yours as you choose it are principles that lie beyond the patterns of your day-to-day living. As the experience within the material world has rules, laws, and principles, so too does the vast environment of your divine nature. Beyond time and space is where the essence of you resides. Consider that only a portion of your conscious awareness is in form. You also exist in light. When you go to sleep at night and as your body rests, you are reunited with the full and integrated experience of your essential Self. The light experience, just as the rest, is highly restorative. Your divine nature re-Sources everything about you. You are a being that resides beyond boundaries.

If you are more than a human being, then who are you? You are multidimensional, you are eternal, you are Source, you are Love. You are never separate from the Source of your being. You are the unique and the Beloved. You are fed by the brilliant ever present, eternal expression of Love. Forever evolving. The process of enlightenment is the process whereby you discover that who you are is and always has been God, Source, Love. There is no separation. You are connected to All, as All is connected to you.

What does this mean? These words have not changed anything of the truth of you. Your days lived thus far have always been lived within the experience of you as Source in form, a being of light in form. Our intention is to support the conscious reconnection of your inner knowing, beyond our words, or the words of any other. Does reading the Bible or any other inspired work, such as this, connect you with the knowing you are eternal? Only you can do the work of you. All we can do is shine light on the path before you, showing you possibility in search of your own heart's resonance. There are thoughts of being eternal, but do you hold the memory of eternal experience?

The resonance of Love is familiar. As you connect with Love, you are led through an internal pathway that is unique unto you.

The intention of this conversation is to support you as you look from an even larger perspective upon your truth. If who you are is Source, then what does that mean? When you begin to look newly, you find newly.

We shift your gaze today to the heavens. Look upon the eternal lights of creation above. Look beside you to the hearts of your brothers and sisters.

Now what, Beloved? We embrace you with the comforting blanket of knowing, of clarity, of peace and of resonance. You are surrounded by God as you are God.

DAY 210: ALLOW ELEVATION

The natural process of enlightenment offers many new avenues of being, perspective, and potential actualized. To move from one perspective to another one must actually move. To attain a new vast perspective of divine order and your space within the sacred, you must elevate. Those present in light today offer the experience of elevation if you so choose.

The process of enlightenment is a process of shifting perspective. As you shift in perspective you begin to see newly. The structure you had thought was iron-clad turns out to be fluid. The value you place on your own being must expand as you begin to see the divine expression that you are. Connected to All, you are Source in form. Your existence resides far beyond time and space. You need to step way back to see these concepts and feel the resonant knowing.

The experience of elevation we speak of today is one of allowing your being to rise with your divine knowing. What perspective must you hold as you accept yourself as a being of light in form, as an eternal, unique expression of Love? Allow your Self to rise within your own divine expression. As you rise within your own divinity, it is an act of the sacred. You align awareness with your essence as Love. Your avenue of communication between your human nature and your divine nature that resides in light is amplified. Likened to connecting one hose to another, the water of your soul travels farther, more precisely and directed.

This is not a piece of homework to be done right now. If you feel you would like to experience elevation, then over the next days, you will have support in the process. You still need to be willing to slightly release another level of constraints that allow this most natural process to occur. This stage of expansion occurs naturally as you embrace the totality of your being. When you begin to feel the influence of the light expression of yourself equally to your physical expression, your perspective is vast. You are informed by your highest knowing.

The experience of elevation is a keystone of enlightenment. There is no way to sidestep the inner processes, experiences, and opportunities for learning. The process of enlightenment is as much about the contrast as it is about the expansion. The contrast in living provides a rich backdrop for learning. This level of learning resides within you as a resonant knowing.

From a higher perspective, attained by elevation you are informed by Love. The joy, fulfillment, and peace of connection feels like home. Welcome home.

All is possible through the eyes of Love. What now?

DAY 211: THE ELEVATED EXPERIENCE

Good afternoon. It is I, Thoth, moving to the forefront of this divine conversation. Your Scribe just said, she can "hardly believe we connect like this on a daily basis." I said, "We feel the same way. The beauty of the connection we hold is beyond compare. It is delightful." The topic today is regarding the elevated experience of enlightenment. Consider that a bird in flight is not judgmental of the capacity she has for elevation and the accompanying vast perspective. Those present in light today are beyond counting. The interest and participation in light far surpasses those named. When Love is expanding, All Love is present.

Elevation is the experience of a perspective that is an aligning of your highest expression in light with your physical experience. It is an opportunity to be informed by a higher knowing you hold naturally. Beyond the daily events, which by themselves are wonderful, an elevated experience holds depth, understanding, and resonant knowing that contribute to your expansive process. The perspective available is not possible beyond a profound aligning with your essential Self. The elevated experience may be felt as moments of profound connection. It may be experienced as a new, never held perspective, beyond the weight of your physical experience. You sense the lightness of your being. As you spend moments in the profound state of elevation, the expansive neural pathways for your divine expression are fortified. The more time you spend in this state, the more moments you will have access to this state and the more your day's moments are informed by your divine knowing.

The elevated experience is an experience of the profound. Your senses are heightened as you soak in the beauty that lies around you. You feel the rhythm of the trees, plants, birds, and other natural beings around you. As you sit amid your environment in nature you feel the inhalation and exhalation of the earth, of the universe, around you. It is a magnified experience of the exalted on earth, combined with the exalted in light. As you feel in rhythm with creation, the perspective now brought to your day has tremendous opportunity to shift, if you allow it. This is a stance within an elevated perspective. Rather than releasing the profound, you look for it now in everything around you. What you look for, you find, and more and more, you are connected with the vast beauty of creation and of the universe. Most importantly, you are reconnected with the truth of you.

Your divine nature is breathtakingly beautiful; magnificence in form. Allow yourself to sit in nature; feel the sway of the branches, listen to the communications of the forest. Movement within stillness.

You are beckoned by Love to the genesis of Love. It is there that we meet.

DAY 212: WITHIN THE PULSE OF CREATION

As we have been speaking of the elevated experience, we expand on that today as a way of being. Those present in light are many, as the concept we speak of is at the essence of creation.

Within an elevated experience you are aligned with your highest expression. Rather than considering a heightened experience as something out of the ordinary, we suggest you change your mind. A heightened experience from the perspective of enlightenment becomes a way of being that in and of itself is then a platform for more. An experience of elevation invites you to the genesis of your being. Within the elevated experience you are connected with the heartbeat of Gaia, of creation. You connect as cohesive participant, not from an observer standpoint. This notes a shift in perspective. So far, the observer perspective holds an empowering stance as it allows distance from the limitations and constraints of your experience from the human standpoint. This shift in perspective is another possibility of your vast expression. Once you hold the knowing, not thinking, but the knowing of your connection with All creation, you feel the pulse of creation that has always been present. You feel your part in the pulse. You become a part of the rhythmic force of creation.

When you experience your Self as part of creation, you are altered. You cannot unknow your connection with All. The bonds of separation are broken! As you experience the sacred connection with All, you are returned to the genesis of Love. You are restored to your alignment with truth.

The Rhythm of Love

The experiences we speak of are not attained through a linear process. They occur first as moments of clarity, moments of breathtaking beauty. Rather than holding something out that you feel you may not attain, we choose rather to show you the truth of your nature. When those moments of exquisite beauty come into your awareness, know that they are indicators of your true nature. Sit in the moment and allow the moment to speak to you. Feel your connection with All, know the moment is about you speaking to you. The divine expression of you seeks realization. If you can, move into the moment, allow your breath to slow as you feel the exquisite air and light around you. Rather than observing, feel your connection with All. Fine-tune your aware-ness, listen to the trees, water, animals, and landscape around you and hear what they are saying. Feel the pulse of life. Feel the pulse of Gaia. Feel the genesis of Love. Trust your knowing.

The enlightened experience is one that occurs from your vast perspective, available as you become less defined by the limitations inherent in the physical. The enlightened experience is one that connects you more deeply not only to the vast awareness of your true nature, but the experience now contributes to everything you see around you in your day. You see beyond boundaries, definitions, and limitations to an experience of the world you live in that is enhanced beyond description. You hold the space of the genesis of Love. You are a Master creator. Your creations now hold the reso-nance of divine expression, aligned with your soul's intention.

As a divine expression of Love, we bathe you in the light of your knowing; anointed with the sacred remembrance of your truth.

DAY 213: TRUST YOUR POSITIONING

As you move your perspective to a more expansive viewpoint, you see the divine design at play around you. You see your relative position to events of your life from a unique vantage point. Those present in light today amplify your clarity in support of your knowing. Moving to the forefront of this divine conversation in harmony, include Jeshua, Melchizadek, Infinite Oneness, Mary Magdalene, Isis, Archangel Michael, Archangel Gabriel, Sanat Kumara, and Abraham.

Embracing your elevated perspective is a process of trust. When you are aligned with your highest expression, you are aligned with your essential Self, and you move with purpose and conscious awareness through the events of your life. When the constraints and limitations of beliefs and habit do not impede your viewpoint, you have access to the highest perspective available to you. This is a part of the enlightenment process. The enlightenment or self-realization process asks you to examine the events of your moments, bringing awareness and conscious choice into action. As your perspective shifts, you succumb to fewer of the limitations and constraints that are inherent in the human experience and begin to create your moments informed by your essence.

The elevated experience of alignment with your essential Self is one that is organic. Just as your heart beats without you thinking it so, your essential Self is at play in each moment. The act of thinking and planning as you have related to it previously is shifted instead to turning toward the wisdom within you that is innate. You are always working within your best interest. As you access more of the wisdom present within your light expression, the connection is beyond thought. Have you found "things working out for you" lately? Have you recognized unforeseen events that bring a new possibility into play, a shift in directions, or a feeling of a "clean slate"? These are part and parcel of the experience of accessing your innate wisdom.

This conscious access into light requests a new level of trust that your heart is beating. Trust your divine expression. Look at things in your life as not happening to you; instead, they happen because of you. You hold a space at the table. This shift in viewpoint asks you to really own your divine expression. What if you recognized the fact you are, in this moment, sitting at the table, beside the divine Masters, whose names you recognize? We meet you eye to eye, peer to peer, divine to divine.

If you could only see what we see, when we look at you. And that is where we are going. The view is magnificent from where we sit.

DAY 214: DIVINE CONSCIOUSNESS

It is within the stillness that you find vibrant expression, only if you can first move through the illusion of activity to find the stillness. This is the conundrum of consciousness. The Masters present in light today contribute the light of their essence as a resonant beacon.

Divine consciousness is the tipping point of awareness that no longer utilizes "difference" as a way of being, and instead turns to inclusion as a basis from which to understand, Be, and create.

This is a subtle distinction to make. Your process of expanding awareness has had you identify the new openings, the expanded ways of being, by referring to or creating a context of "different." You utilized your experience from the past to judge what was occurring in your process of becoming untethered from the constraints held by your past, belief systems, habits, and patterns.

Consciousness holds a variety of possible vantage points from which to create your life. Today, we offer the possibility of divine consciousness. This is a perspective whereby you already view yourself as the divine, the sacred, the Beloved, a being connected to All. From this perspective you are All, you are Love.

This distinction makes possible a reorienting, a reframing of you as a divine being of light in form; Source in form. Said another way, this is as a tipping point between being a human being having a spiritual experience, and being a spiritual being having a human experience. When you shift your perspective to the latter, what then becomes possible? This viewpoint holds you in alignment with your divine design. You are empowered within your day's moments, and you are at choice consciously.

Divine consciousness is another step over the threshold of awareness. When you step over the threshold, your life becomes on purpose and in alignment with your very essence. Your experience in all facets of your life is enhanced as you live through the lens of Love. It is a game changer.

Today we place on the altar for your consideration the possibility of Divine Consciousness.

DAY 215: HOLDING WHOLENESS

As you embrace the consciousness of your divine expression you also hold All in wholeness. There is nothing needing to be added, fixed, or subtracted for perfection to emanate.

Bringing one's consciousness into alignment with divine expression holds an elevated, vast perspective. This is a state of being that is beyond your thinking. This is a state of being that oversees your thinking. This is a state of being so deep there is no distinction or possibility that exists beyond that of perfection and alignment with the divine expression that you are in your essential Self.

This is an experience that has been sought by many and attained after much meditation and inner reflection. And it is also available for you as a possibility. What this means for your day's moments is you develop a new frame of reference. Your frame of reference becomes one of wholeness of everything, everyone, and every situation. There is nothing to be fixed, changed, maneuvered. All is perfect in this Now immaculate moment. All there is, is Love. The being of Love is a powerful catalyst of transformation. As you BE Love from the perspective of wholeness, you restore to wholeness. Your creative abilities are at their peak as you view wholeness. From this perspective you transform through the fine vibrations of wholeness that you emanate. Your fine frequency field of Love is a powerful force for joy, clarity, truth, and manifestation.

As you choose to manifest from this perspective, you choose without the presence of need or want. You choose because you choose. Nothing more. You choose as a reflection of the divine expression of Love that you are. Your creations and manifestations on the physical plane are available to you. You will find your field already holds the abundance and creations in your field from many lifetimes of accumulation. All available to you as you choose. When you raise your frequency, your vibrational field, to that of Love and wholeness, you are not re-creating the element of needing or wanting. You create from Love, *period.*

Your perspective from the space of wholeness is one of Love and compassion. As you view all people around you as whole, you hold open the space for their realization of that state. As you hold others in a space of limitation, you support the creation of that too. This is a process that is a discipline. Learning to be aligned with your highest expression is a most rewarding life's work. It is something that lives in the background of your thoughts and moments. You do the work of a Master while at the grocery store, cleaning your home, and planting in your garden.

What we speak of is a transformative, catalytic, potent way of being. Beyond the limitations and constraints of your thinking and beliefs lies a reality of the extraordinary; it is heaven. Heaven on earth. You are where heaven and earth meet. You are All.

DAY 216: WHOLENESS BEYOND CIRCUMSTANCE

W hen wholeness is chosen as a backdrop of living, there are times where, in living the breadth of the gradient of light expression that you are, you will notice something that appears, by all tests, to be broken, not aligned, and even not of Love. We take another step back in perspective today to reveal the larger truth. It is in Love and delight that we gather on this beautiful day, as reflection of your exquisite expression within the All. Those also moving to the forefront of today's conversation include Abraham, Infinite Oneness, Mary Magdalene, Buddha, Legions of Light, the Hathors, Isis, Archangel Michael, Jeshua, Golden Stargate, and Sai Baba.

The gathering in light is vast today. This perspective, often gained after years, even lifetimes, of reflection, is one that joins heaven and earth. Based within the light of Love always, there is a point of view that when achieved is clearly seen as nothing but the divine perfection of All. So far within the matrix of *In Service to Love*, we have shone the light, so you may step back to see newly. As each level of awareness opens, there is a new perspective that becomes available. When one is standing "up close" to a situation or event, this perspective is not available. Conscious awareness is about con-tinually adjusting your awareness to see "the more" that is present in each immaculate moment. As you experience the knowing through your resonant response, you are reunited with facets of your divine expression. You begin to see, hear, and discern the voice of your soul as joy, peace, beauty, compassion, Love, and clarity moves into your view. It is only when you experience the new perspective that you see the truth available at each step. You see the truth of the appearance of separation, you see the illusion of division, and then beyond that you see the resonant, eternal light of Love and how the light of Love shines on All.

When you see a plant in your garden in summer, you see and feel the vibrance, the color, the fragrance, how the light is reflected off the velvet petals. In the winter, beyond your view, the flower remains alive. It has never left. The flower remains in the seed, in the tuber, within the soil, gathering sustenance for the next season of brilliant display. So it is, with those issues, events, or even people you view as separate, absent, unconscious, less than Love. The events and people are in a much larger eternal play where, within the ebb and flow of life's expression, wholeness is always present. Only seen by those who choose to see newly, the resonant knowing is a gift of your divine essence. Love flows eternally, beyond circumstance. When the stance of wholeness is held in your moments, the beauty that is ever present is revealed. In the sheer act of holding the viewpoint of wholeness, the process of enlightenment is supported, as when you water a plant that has been parched so it may return to its most vibrant expression. The expression of wholeness is ever present.

The perspective of wholeness aligns you as well to the divine perfection of you. The vast expanse of your true nature is revealed only through the inner knowing. Guided by inner knowing you are led to the wholeness that exists within you. From your new perspective, you feel the cohesion, the unity, the heartbeat of the exalted, eternal divine moving through your very cells and within the air you breathe.

The broader the perspective you hold, the more you are acting within the greater and greater components of light that is your eternal expression. More and more, you align with your highest knowing.

The perspective of wholeness is potent. Based in the light of Love, this point of view holds alchemical qualities. Hold the intention of a perspective of wholeness even as you notice you slip out of it. Return to the vast perspective that is your very nature. As you spend more of your moments in this exalted space, the clarity, joy, peace, and abundance that is your nature also comes into view. It must be so.

We shine the light for your vast expression made manifest. We remain In Service to Love.

DAY 217: LIVING INFORMED BY WHOLENESS

When wholeness is held as the background to your living, it informs your every decision. Your creating is elevated as it draws upon the highest truth of you. You are whole. Whether in light or in form you are never ever anything other than perfection, wholeness, connected to All. Those present today bring clarity and ease with the transition to this as a way of being as you choose.

Where we sit at this moment we are surrounded by tall evergreen trees. If you were to walk up to the tree and put your nose near the tree you would feel the thickness and texture of the bark. From that you would be able to tell the life force of the tree. The girth of the tree gives you an idea of the age; you may see some branches with needles and smell the fragrance of the oils of the tree. It is not until you step back many yards that you can look up and get an idea of the height of the tree. It is only when you stand back that you see the tree in its wholeness. When you stand up close, you have an experience of the tree in part. Viewing yourself in wholeness requires you stand way back beyond definitions you have assigned from the past.

When you stand back and intend to hold a vast perspective that holds wholeness, it is only then that you are not distracted by the specifics of the details of life; you see from a perspective that holds more information. The perspective of wholeness, again, is a practice first initiated through intent. As you choose to see newly, you will. It is at that point a new vista opens before you. The majesty of the whole picture informs you beyond the details of any given situation. Automatically the "barbs" or "hooks" that have held you as limited may be released. We are spending several days upon this topic as it brings the paradigm shift required to disentangle yourself from the issues that hold you as stuck. This is a key to the door and next expression that lies before you.

When wholeness is held as a "tactic" to a particular end, it will fall flat. When wholeness is guided by the inner resonance you hold, it is a next stage for your exploration. The distinction we make here is, if there is an agenda that states "I will look at wholeness to gain access to my abundance," what you are in fact saying is, "I am separate from my abundance." And the abundance you seek will be illusory. When you choose wholeness because you choose wholeness as a step in the path to your enlightenment, your experience will be one that is sourced by your wholeness. Do you see the difference in the two approaches? Wherever there is lack, you are not being informed by wholeness, you are being informed by separation. As you move into wholeness as attainment of your highest expression and all it entails, the door to all your abundance is open and then becomes a choice that is unfettered.

As we move with you in the experience of increasingly expansive light expression, the beingness that informs your choices and decisions requires conscious awareness. Today we shine light on the background way of being that informs the choices and perspectives held in your life.

It is with Love and delight that we point to the potency and magnitude of your divine expression.

Day 218: The Power of Choice Within Wholeness

How does one frame choice within the background way of being as wholeness? It would seem when you choose one thing, you say no to another. Is that an act of separation? We would ask you to consider the power of choice within the background of wholeness.

As you hold the way of being as wholeness, wholeness directs all your thoughts, questions, and actions. Consider that you already hold a background way of being. The background way of being, whatever it is, informs all your choices. If the color blue, for example, is a way of being, then colors other than shades of blue will not be a fit for your referencing. In this case, as you hold a background way of being as wholeness, the wholeness would refer to all those frequencies, relationships, thoughts, and actions, whether conscious or unconscious, that are in alignment with your highest expression. With each intention and action in alignment with your highest expression, or not, you communicate a trajectory.

Your divine nature holds unique qualities, purpose, and design. Within your divine design and plan for this lifetime, you hold a template, or ultimate intention, that supports your totality within the evolutionary process. Fulfilling your highest purpose for this life is fulfilling wholeness for you and is ultimately a contribution to the expression of Love and All. A rose in the garden has specific needs; good soil, watering, pruning, fertilizing. A redwood in the forest has a different requirement, left only to the seasons. Your specific needs that support your ultimate divine expression is your expression of wholeness. As you honor you, you honor All.

Choice also delineates boundaries. Boundaries are the edges of your life experience when aligned with your intention, and they identify areas of incompatibility. Have you noticed a shift of people in your life, in either your job or personal life? Some people will transition into your life and others are no longer active participants in your days? As your state of consciousness shifts, the reality is reflected in your life. You see the effect of your state of consciousness in your environment. The farther you move on your gradient of light expression, the more you make choices that affirm your direction. As you say yes to wholeness, those things, thoughts, events, and people that don't support your highest expression no longer hold the same resonance. If from the perspective of this Now moment the resonance is no longer present, and you find yourself struggling to release, you send a bit of a "wobble," or contradiction signal. Consider that if someone's presence no longer resonates with you, your presence also no longer resonates with them. Consider that the struggle does not lie in the test of resonance; the struggle lies in an emotion or belief component where there is a conflict. The appearance or feeling of conflict is a valuable tool to gaining clarity and restoring velocity.

As you choose to change and expand your level of awareness, expect movement in all areas of your life. As you move your conscious awareness to the root of all your choices, you will conclude you are informed moment to moment by your divine expression. As you choose wholeness as a background way of being, you support your highest expression beyond the agendas of any other way of being. Wholeness is informed by Love. For Love is all there is.

The choice for wholeness is a choice for Love as revealed through your divine unique expression. Only you hold the design of you. You are the key to all the universes and all the knowing there ever was, is, and ever will be. You hold the eternal flame of Love.

DAY 219: IN COLLABORATION WITH YOUR DIVINE ESSENCE

G ood evening, Beloveds. It is on this most auspicious day we greet you. It is I, Thoth, moving to the forefront of this divine conversation within this Now immaculate moment. As we have been speaking of wholeness, we refer to the totality of you. If you would, imagine the totality of the gradient of light expression. This incorporates you as a being of light in form and the expression of you that resides in light. We have been speaking of the shift from being informed from external sources, patterns, and default systems to being internally referenced. We speak of your divine nature informing your human nature. The separation between form and light dissipates as you contemplate the wholeness of you. The wholeness of you is both form and light. So again, rather than inferring that the light expression is outside of you and somehow you are trying to reach it, within the realm of wholeness you already are connected, as your arm is connected to your shoulder. Not separate, but part of the whole. Those present in light contributing to this conversation delight in the reality of you connecting consciously with your highest expression and drawing upon the nectar of divine wisdom that is innately yours. Moving to the forefront of this divine conversation are Jeshua, Mary Magdalene, Infinite Oneness, St. Germain, Melchizadek, St. Augustine, Abraham, Isis, and Archangel Michael.

As you listen to music, you recognize that the sound you hear is a series of notes joined in varying cadences and tones. Included in the music, behind the music, is the space between the notes. The space between the notes, albeit brief, is the silence that gives texture and emotion to the music that you hear. Today we speak of the relationship between you as a being of light in form and the access you hold to your highest expression. We use the analogy of music to demonstrate the omnipresent state of your expression that resides in light. Your moments in form may be likened to the notes you hear. The voice of your soul is at the helm as the silence that laces the notes of the music together. The silence directs the notes. Do you begin to get a sense of the pervasive presence of your divine expression? We utilize the implication of separation to denote a process. In fact, your divine expression is ever present, and never has been nor will be separate. You are a cohesive divine expression of Love. Since you are omnipresent, you may consider that all parts of you are readily available.

How does this communication, that already takes place, often on an unconscious level, become conscious? As you begin to evolve your awareness to consider the wholeness of you, you create an opening for the expansive expression of your authentic nature to come into view. From that consideration of the possibility of realizing your totality you stand at the water's edge of your being and allow the fog of illusion to rise, revealing the brilliance of your eternal nature. Imagine the music. Listen for the silence behind the notes of your day. Feel the presence that steers your moments. As you fine-tune your senses to receive the impulses of light from your highest expression, you tap into your divine wisdom.

The voice of your soul is pervasive, as opposed to a singular impulse that would be likened to a musical note. The way you receive information from your highest expression is through fields of awareness, much in the way this work is transduced and received by your Scribe. She receives impulses of light and consciousness in full concepts, then transcribes the field into words upon her keyboard. So, recognize that the way you receive information internally is natural. You do it all the time. The process of bringing this to your conscious awareness is listening and feeling newly to begin to identify a field of awareness that is always present with you, behind the notes of your day.

Listen for your silent, ever present symphony. The music behind the music of your day. Begin to sense the field of awareness that you occupy. When you connect, you will sense the celebration of the heavens.

DAY 220: SURRENDERING TO UNITY

Good evening, Beloveds. It is I, Thoth, moving to the forefront of this divine conversation within this Now immaculate moment. When you feel separate, surrender to unity. Those present today shine light on the truth of your eternal expression. There is never a time when you are not connected, deeply, unrelentingly, inextricably, eternally connected to All that is. You are an eternal expression of Love; how could you ever actually be separate? In support of your divine remembering, those stepping to the forefront of this conversation include Jeshua, Mary Magdalene, Archangel Michael, Archangel Gabriel, Melchizadek, Metatron, Legions of Light, and the Hathors.

Those present today all bring vast histories, experiences, and knowing. Each uniquely embodies the wisdom of Love. Within the experience of unique expression, there is the common knowledge of unity. When one makes the choice for embodiment into form, there is the need to narrow expression to the physical realms. There is a descent into the illusion of separation.

For you, the movement into illusion's experience is not the end. For many lifetimes you have sought the divine knowing you feel in the outer reaches of memory. You have hungered for the connection you know as truth. This has been an eternal questioning of "Who am I?" We have presented concepts that require an ever-expanding perspective to occur. It is through the velocity of your inquiry that the actualization of enlightenment is at hand as possibility. A realization whose time has come.

As you surrender to unity, the constructs that hold you as separate dissipate. As the veil of illusion is lifted, you hold the stance of living in many realms. You consciously receive sustenance from the heavens available to all who seek beyond the illusion of separation.

The knowing beyond illusion connects you with your highest expression while you are in form. You hold the opportunity in every moment to be informed by the voice of your soul. Your experience is being more of you.

We ask you to consider the reality of connection beyond separation. Who would you have to be?

DAY 221: THE PROFOUND
OPPORTUNITY AT HAND

Good evening. It is I, Thoth, moving to the forefront of this divine conversation within this Now immaculate moment. The opportunity that is embraced by the Now moment is unlimited. Within the process of *In Service to Love* we hold high the full-on expression of your soul, made manifest within your day's moments, consciously.

The process of enlightenment is the alignment of your divine nature with your human nature. The awareness you hold in light becomes available while you are in form, beyond perceived boundaries of time and space. What if those profound moments you treasure were a peek through the veil to the truth of you? What if you could access consciously the wisdom held by your soul? There is a treasure trove available within the choice for aligning with your highest truth. The energy available today and through to the completion of Day 244 contains light infusion, activations, and in some cases consciousness downloads to support the alignment of your highest expression. Again, as you choose. This is a Master class, led by Masters. The opportunity at hand is the clarity of connection and communion with the highest expressions available in light. You chose the path of Love, the path of expansion, long before you came into form in this life. The work we do together is in the creation of an environment that supports that which you have already chosen, in discovery of that which already exists as your authentic nature. Those present also stepping to the forefront of this divine conversation include Jeshua, Isis, Melchizadek, Sanat Kumara, the Hathors, Legions of Light, Archangel Michael, Archangel Gabriel, Mary Magdalene, Mother Mary, and St. Germain.

As you sit within the rich environment of silence, you begin to feel the presence of your divine expression. You begin to feel the presence of who you are in light, extended into form. The manifestation of Love that you BE is profound. What if you are led by All that you BE? What if your humanity became fully conscious? And then what? And what of divine collaboration? What is possible as your expression within divine collaboration?

The Masters in light are present still, available in each moment. The words held within spiritual and religious texts have survived for their ring of truth. They are products of the past. What could be possible Now, as you are met eye to eye, peer to peer, and divine to divine?

What becomes possible in Love?

Day 222: What If?

What if you could live your heart's desire? What would that be? Where would you begin? The time is at hand. It is with deep joy and delight that we greet you tonight. We see the leaps of faith, we see the light expanded, we see the voice of your soul, as the echoes reach beyond the abyss of time and space to your heart. We see the light of your being emanate in divine radiance.

What is it that is held so deeply in your heart that you dare not even give voice to it? What is your greatest dream? As you move to the end moments of this life, what is it you would have wanted most? As you gaze into the moments of crystal clarity during the inter-life, you realize that in the here and now, in this Now moment, your greatest of heart's desires are possible.

The contribution you choose to be occurs as you BE more of you. As you gain access to the awareness you hold, that was previously only in light, there is an amplifying of the expression of you. With each choice that is made that is in alignment with your highest expression, the propensity increases for more of your highest expression birthed into form. The spark of resonance and expansion develops velocity. It's like being on a skating rink; with each skate's stroke, you gain speed, ease, and velocity.

What if the voice of your soul brings an integral note to the divine opus? What if only your gaze could reignite someone's hope? What if the potency of Love you hold is the link that catalyzes peace?

What if the voice of your soul lands?

DAY 223: FOR THE JOY OF IT

The opportunity you hold while in form is magnificent. The feeling of the warm breeze on your face, the sun's embrace of summer's eve, the colors of sky as the clouds and light play upon the canvas above. Enjoyed, reveled within, those are the gifts of the experience in form. Just for the joy of it all.

As we point to different aspects in the process of enlightenment, it is easy to collapse attention to that which is your soul's ultimate intention. Today we move your attention to the gifts that are at hand. Nothing to be done, no problems to solve, your choice for experience in form was a choice for the opportunity of everything the experience in form has to offer. The experience of being incarnate is the foreground against which the background of intention is painted. As you connect more deeply with the divine expression that is solely yours, the experiences of physical state become heightened. The limitations of form are no longer seen as barriers, instead, appreciated for all they are, and all they are not. The experience of wholeness has an orientation that allows the totality to be seen. From the vast perspective, All is appreciated.

The gift of being, in the present moment allows the saturation of experience in the beauty of form. Experienced through your body, the voice of God is heard in the wonder of the eternal mystery.

Beloved, be present in your life's moments. They are transient, and vanish in the blink of an eye. Follow your heart's calling and revel in the magic—just for the fun of it.

Day 224: Contrast, a Platform for Life

As you examine the components of your life, you see there are areas, periods of time, events, that are indelibly marked in your memory. The full ripple effect of these occurrences are often below your awareness. In the shock of a trauma, pain and difficult events you make an unconscious decision. The decision stays present in your experience as a background influence on future choices. Rather than hurry up and move past the difficult moments, we bring them to wholeness. The events of your life that represented a challenge are in fact potent milestones from the perspective of evolutionary growth. Those present today, in witness to the return to wholeness, include Jeshua, St. Francis, St. Germain, Archangel Michael, Archangel Gabriel, Mary Magdalene, Melchizadek, and Isis.

You know by now the powerful opportunity for learning that is available with the experience of contrast. What we speak of today is the residue of those events. The residual shock, reaction, and shutdown hold a limiting quality, a sense of "I won't do that again," or an over-correction. With each decision to limit your expression in reaction to events, consider that your self-perception became more limited. As you become aware of your beliefs created in reaction, there is an understanding that becomes available. Today we look at the restoration of wholeness. A claim consciously of the you that is unlimited in every way.

We would like you to consider the realms in which you store information related to events of your life. There are energetic fields around you and within parts of your body that hold on to energetic reaction. It may be likened to a rush of adrenaline in your body, when you are startled or immediately on alert. The residual energetic "cloud" is held in your field even though there may have been an understanding or healing, or a passing of time lessening the experience of pain. Today and through to the completion of *In Service to Love Book 2: Love Elevated,* we support you through an infusion of light that reintegrates areas of you that were separated through pain, trauma, and shock. These moments of pain are not to be reexperienced or activated; instead they are lovingly returned to wholeness.

The experience of wholeness is the platform for the next levels of expansion of conscious awareness. The events of pain, although they may have occurred decades ago, become diminished mentally and emotionally; however, in many cases your energetic field has held on to the constriction. Today, the restrictions from past traumas are released and returned to the whole. This is an integration, not a removal. As right and wrong have shifted in perspective to that of unity, so too is the experience of pain not erased, but returned to the All. The benefit for you is an experience of a release where a deep breath may be taken.

The areas of contrast and pain in your life may be utilized and recycled to lift you to your next level of awareness. As your experience of pain, discomfort, and challenge are reused, they are no longer swept under the rug, ignored, or avoided. They are honored and returned to the whole where they contribute to your next steps.

Unhindered by past limitations, another layer is released, returning you to your expansive expression. Like rungs on a ladder, each step becomes a platform for the next step.

It is in Love we bathe you, Beloved, in the comforting light of restoration. Making possible a birthing into yet another reality.

DAY 225: LED BY LOVE

As you move toward expansion of your awareness, you connect with your essential Self. You begin to see your own divine expression as you experience the resonance and affirmation of truth. Your life becomes altered in that you are adjusting to what it means now, as you align consciously with your divine nature. How does that make your life different? You, Beloved, are the key. Your contribution to Love may be opened only by you. You are the contribution of Love.

Your energetic presence expands as you zero in on the divine expression that is you. Have you noticed your shifting energetic pattern? The potency of your being reflects the deeper, more consistent access to the expression of Love and your authentic nature. You are being informed consistently by the larger perspective governed by your essence. If you are Love, then what is the predictable outcome? More Love. This is not something you do. This is a way of being that shifts as you contemplate your truth and release the limitations of a lower-frequency experience. The parameters of your life shift to reflect the expansive awareness you now hold.

You become led by your soul. You become in service to Love. Love, in service to Love. If the meaning of the world as you know it is run by limited perceptions, then with the absence of those perceptions, what else is left on the table? Indeed, it is Love. The basis of All. Your expression of Love is perfectly you. What this looks like is more joy, more freedom, clarity and sense of purpose. You still have events in your life that are in contrast, but now they may be viewed through the lens of process rather than limitation.

Your Scribe has noticed the sense of purpose in her days, being led to events at specific times to witness what is there. From the space of witness, there is an opportunity to be led by Love to those moments that make a difference either for you or for someone else. Transformation in the blink of an eye.

Realize that your expansion hearkens to a new way of being. This is not business as usual. There is nothing usual about the profound within the immaculate Now moment. It opens the space of witness to the sacred.

Settle into your new space of your perfect expression of Love. Follow the joy in your heart. Allow the voice of your soul, your divine expression of Love, to lead you. And so it begins.

DAY 226: AUTHENTICITY AND POTENCY

Good evening, Beloveds. It is I, Thoth, stepping to the fore-front of this divine conversation as translated by your Scribe, Darlene. The process within which our conversations are trans-duced, translated, and received is one of authentic expression. The essential expression of Darlene is many things, and one facet displays an adeptness in translating light, frequency, and conscious-ness. This is a potent quality. You too have authentic expressions that hold the highest level of potency. Today, we speak in unison as the Council of Light.

Potency provides clarity, strength, and integrity and is available as you release limitations that are not in alignment with your highest expression. Emotions such as worry, doubt, and concern may also move through Darlene; however, it is the increasing potency of her authentic expression that continues to eclipse other concerns. There was a time when the concerns eclipsed the confidence to pursue what is her highest expression. Consider there has also been a play or a dance that you have created around your own divine nature and the full-on expression of it. It is not as though you must do something to be fulfilled in this life. It is more that the fulfil-ment you seek within the deepest reaches of your soul is found in the treasure chest of your divine nature. The process of expanding consciousness is one that incorporates layers of awareness revealed through the clarity of new perspectives. New viewpoints identify

limitations and inauthenticity. Once identified, new levels of awareness surface, shedding light and ultimately aligning you more perfectly with the divine expression you are. The clarity in alignment
with your highest expression brings with it a new level of potency.

As you gain new levels of potency there are many more layers of your expression that come into play. As you continue to
step back and see new perspectives, you gain confidence that
the new perspectives are available. There is always more. In pur-
suing the "more" the veil is pulled back, revealing a new vision
of you. Rather than being an argument for the justification of
the way you have viewed life previously, you continue to choose
ways of being in your life that align closely with your essential
Self. Inauthenticity becomes foreign, and its presence brings discomfort. Behavior and ways of being that used to exist below the
surface of your awareness become glaring in limitations that no
longer fit.

With each choice that is in alignment with your highest expression you open the door for potential realized that was not available in the presence of limitation. Each new awareness reveals the
unimaginable. Like the snowball rolling downhill, you gain speed,
momentum, and velocity in your process of expansion. With each
step forward, your potency of being increases. The clarion call of
your being is heard.

DAY 227: EMBODIMENT OF THE DIVINE

Good evening, Beloveds. It is with delight that I, Thoth, step forward in this divine conversation within this Now immaculate moment. Those present in light carry the message of divine Love and remembrance of your highest expression. Present in our gathering today are Mary Magdalene, Jeshua, Infinite Oneness, Isis, Archangel Gabriel, Archangel Michael, Melchizadek, Mother Mary, and St. Germain.

We have been speaking of the continual aligning with your divine nature as the integral component of enlightenment. The true process of expanding consciousness is further described as the embodiment of you, by you: the embodiment of the divine. If you were to view a picture of a tree on a postcard, the beauty is apparent and inspiring. As you embody your Self, the process may be likened to comparing the tree on the postcard to the experience to standing within the giant redwood forest, embraced by the boughs, reveling in their vitality, experiencing the rich fragrances and the knowing of the grandeur. You embodying you is enlightenment, as there is the actualization of no separation between you in form and you in light. You are divinity extended into form. From your physical perspective you are divinity experiencing Self. You are Source experiencing Self. What may be gained from the focus to continually see newly in order to realize the divinity that is you? You BE in the world, but not of it. Your awareness is beyond limitations of form. Your gift to the world of matter is the divine light you bring to bear within your presence. A process sought by few that holds untold treasures.

It is I, Mary Magdalene, stepping to the forefront in this Now immaculate moment. As you embrace the divine expression of you, the gifts you hold of Love, grace, and compassion that are your authentic nature are crystal clear expressions of your being as you walk your moments in form. You are a conduit for Love, as Love. Even the term heaven on earth implies a separation that is bridged. In fact, you are heaven and earth, in wholeness. What I suggest to you is the immaculate presence you make available in your being is a gift not only for the experiencing of it, but as transformative alchemy. If you are drawn to the highest expression of your being, present in form, we are here dear sister, dear brother. We support you and revel in your perfection in any choice. Many of you reading these words have chosen to come to the earth at this time as guardians of Love, such as Darlene. Guardians of a new era of Love. You are on the leading edge of this both ancient and contemporary realization. The process of enlightenment is not meant only for those who choose a life of solitude and meditative practice. It is a process available to all who choose it. Your moments have drawn you here to this moment. Know you are supported within this most dynamic, expansive, divine collaborative work of *In Service to Love*. Beyond the words within this work is the potent catalyzing force of creation. Love at the spark of creation is where All is possible. This is the conception of this work. It took many lifetimes in the creating and planning and one second to recognize the truth. If you are resonating with the divine embodiment of you by you, know you are held in Love, you are heard, and your journey is a brilliant one.

Your joy, your freedom, your well-being resides in the connection with and access to your most high divine expression. There are many ways to the ultimate expression; this is but one that is available to you if you so choose. No timelines, no hurry-up-and-decide. Place the thought of you embodying you on the altar of inquiry. Ask for clarity. After all, this is a process that occurs from the inside out, not from the outside in. It is a process that is governed by you only. If there is resonance, or the ring of familiarity, ask for clarity. The knowing now is not from the thinking part of your being; it is the experience of resonance. When you are aligned with your highest expression, there is a felt sense of resonance.

We hold you in Love, compassion, and reverie that comes only from the divine recognition of the divine.

DAY 228: ENGAGE LOVE

I t is with delight we convene today. We gather in the name of Love. As you release the limitations inherent in the physical experience, hold on to Love. Love contains all you need and ever wanted. Everything but Love is an empty chalice. Shiny perhaps, but empty.

When you first were born into the life of the physical, you were taught the ways of the world. In general, the conversations of youth are around limitations, not the realms of possibility that exceeds the limitations of form. This is the purpose, however, of the journey of conscious awareness. Your divine nature is revealed within your expanding awareness. The truth of you, as Love, gleams.

Lean on Love. Allow Love to work in your life. When you choose to release your hold on the way life should look, you open the door to the possibility that resides within your essential Self. As the restrictions of form are released, engage Love. When you allow Love to move within your life, you activate a potent catalyzing creative force. When you allow the Love that you are and the Love within All creation to support you, you are living harmoniously.

Recently, when your Scribe was experiencing loss, she was experiencing a sense of constriction. This is a common reaction to the pain of loss; a reflexive holding on tighter to the world you think you know and can rely upon. We say to you the words we relayed to Darlene: "Engage Love." This is not engage "in" Love. Engage Love. As you engage Love, you fall back in Love with the ease and joy that is the hallmark of your soul's essence. Love releases the grip of fear and provides a backdrop for your life to happen within. Allow Love to wash the pain of loss and fear, restoring your freedom and vitality.

Love leads you effortlessly, dancing across the waters of your life in ecstatic expression. Allow the words to be heard and allow the resonant tone to communicate to you.

Engage Love.

Engage Love.

Dearest Beloved, engage Love.

DAY 229: LOVE ETERNAL

As the dimensional realities you reside within are bridged with your conscious awareness, there is no-thing that is outside of your awareness. The concept of the absence of limitations requires a new orientation to your perspective. Those present in light contribute their signature energy, reminding you of the eternal yet ever-changing, evolving nature you hold.

What if every moment of your life spoke deeply? What if your connection to All was experienced in your day? What if fear was replaced with the knowing of your vast divine expression? We communicate these questions today to open a new space of expression. As you reach into the light of your essential nature, the perceived limitations, edges, and boundaries soften, and you move into the space of knowing. As awareness of your true nature expands, the doors open wide to that which is the source of joy, truth, and divine expression.

The experience of the vast knowing of your divine nature is one that does not require "doing," action, or even understanding. The experience of the nonlinear, fluid, broad expression of your truth becomes one that is no longer sought; it becomes one that becomes a way of your being. The pieces and parts are no longer disparate; they are reflections of the facets of you that coexist within your divine nature.

We support in light your awareness of your limitless, eternal nature. Your I AM. Possible within the Now immaculate moment, as you touch upon the divine sacred nature of your truth, you move beyond all perceived limitations and become your greatest knowing, your greatest joy. Love's eternal song.

DAY 230: BEING THE DIVINE EMBODIED

W hen one is informed by the highest expression available, there is an adjusting of access points that is called for. This evening we speak of the access points required to fully give voice to your essence. Those on the Council of Light present this evening support a recalibration of your unique expansion process.

Within the process of accessing more of the light expression that is your nature, there is a shifting perspective from which to BE during your day. Consider that your conscious awareness of the expression of you in light is expanding. Within a moving landscape of the process of enlightenment, there is a shift in your way of being that occurs seemingly organically. The differences in you show up as your attention is drawn to new things during your day. Your way of being as you expand your conscious awareness must shift. Much of this process is seamless. We bring this to your attention today to consciously observe your access points. Is your conscious awareness showing up in your life in your ways of being? Are your relationships shifting or being contributed to? Are you authentic in your moments? Are you feeling more of the potency of your essence?

We speak of the access points today. Access points are the avenues or thresholds over which awareness in light is transported and conveyed and ultimately expressed in your physical reality. If you are accessing more of your expression in light, then who you Be must change. When you expand your awareness in light, you may look beyond your physical reality into that which is formless. The awareness attained in light may also contribute to your physical world. However, the access point for movement into form must shift. To demonstrate, we use the analogy of a hose. A garden hose when turned on delivers water from within the plumbed system to an outside location. If the nozzle on the end of the hose is turned to a setting that does not allow the water to come out, the access to the water in the first place becomes moot because it is not being transported according to the original design of the hose. It's much the same as how awareness attained in light can make a difference in your physical reality when you turn the setting on yourself (the nozzle) to reflect the expanding access to light and conscious awareness.

Another example: If you are attaining a lot of light awareness, you must shift your way of being in the world to match the new expanded state. One way this is accomplished is through an awareness of "taking your place," not just at the table, but staking claim to your ownership of All of you, demonstrated within your life Now. As you "own" the new potent expression of you, your presence shifts in potency. Be clear this is not a "power" expression, although it will be an expression of empowerment. It is not power obtained through control. The expression we refer to is "*You undiluted.*" You have adapted to ways of discounting or hiding your brilliance. We ask you to consider looking a bit closer to your physical expression and see if the potency you express during your day is authentically matched with the potency of your Self. This will bring a recalibration of your access and expression of your authentic divine nature. The conscious adjusting of your access points in light and in form will align your awareness and expression.

We remind you to fill the divine golden slippers of your awareness. This feels organic as you release more of the limitations of your perception of yourself in the physical world. Who you are is Source extended into form. Wholeness, integration of your human nature with your divine nature, is the highest expression of authenticity available.

Day 231: The Season's Change

As the summer's warmth shifts to the crisp air that announces the coming of fall, so too do you have seasons in your expansive process of conscious awareness. We were speaking of the access points you utilize to accommodate expansive awareness.

Over the years of your incarnation you have amassed a vast library of information in the ways of being and doing that support the endeavors of your choice. Your learning began with family and extended to school and friendships and then led to independence and the creation of your life's trajectory based upon choices made. The learning process requires that levels of mastery be attained that open the doors to more possibilities. The understanding of access points brings to light awareness you have attained to this point and creates an opening for the full expression of you, allowing you to create in your life from the music of your soul.

Even in this moment there is a shift in the way information is accessed by your Scribe. The clarity of access points is presented to her in support of attaining a new level of mastery in moving the information of our conversations from light into form. The access point is a term we have given the doorway or threshold through which your knowing in light, the melody of your soul, may be translated and moved into form.

As you move into different phases of your life, new ways of being are naturally called upon. The concept of access points is one that facilitates the amplification of your soul's voice. This awareness brings about consciousness around manifestation. Understand that this is a natural and organic process. You already have utilized access points in your life, but they have for the most part existed below your conscious awareness. We bring them to light in this conversation.

Utilize Access Points

An access point is an avenue that brings the awareness attained in light into form. It is a shift of awareness that utilizes action. Awareness in light already exists in light, so how will the light awareness result in manifestation in the physical? First, as your awareness expands, there is a natural shift in your energy or your way of being. There is a vitality that is present and a sense of action that has momentum.

The way you bring light into form is through your being and in your action. As you are now more informed by your highest expression rather than being informed by the limitations and definitions, you experience resonance. Resonance communicates alignment with your I AM Self. Once you experience resonance you can allow that to direct you into action. As an example, an artist must spend time in front of the canvas in the process of moving inspiration, found in light, into form on the canvas.

Access Point of Inspiration *Resonance inspires being. The artist is inspired. You hear the voice of your soul. Inspiration without action, is but a beautiful moment.*

Access Point of Action *Inspiration requests expression. The artist places paintbrush in hand and sits in front of the canvas. You bring action to the inspiration, joining light and form. Action without inspiration is empty.*

Beloveds, the song of your soul holds inspiration and divine design seeking expression. The resonance you experience is the clay for creation. Where may you open an access point to write the music of the heavens and craft your masterpiece?

DAY 232: FROM LIGHT TO FORM

Conscious awareness reveals what was hidden from view. The natural organic process of evolutionary expansion has always existed; we bring to light the expansive abilities you hold naturally as a being of light in form. So far, our conversations have been directed toward movement beyond the physical into the deeper realms of light, awareness, and access. As the tide turns and the seasons change, we shift our attention to the action of moving wisdom of your divine nature into the physical realm.

The awareness you hold naturally is vast. Through the density of the veil of physical reality, the knowing in light is experienced often as unreachable, or perhaps seen only in brief glimpses. The access points of inspiration and action are activated through resonance that comes from your highest knowing. Many stop at the natural phenomenon of the divine, deeply touched by the beauty of the moment, and miss the opportunity available for inspired action. Many feel the internal fulfillment of divine access, inspiration, healing, and comfort and protect it as a cherished sacred moment. What if the profound beauty of the divine moment was a doorway to more of you?

Just as there is always more, there is only another shift in the facets of your awareness that allows that which is received and accessed from your most divine nature to flow into the physical realm. Once you can identify those limitations and barriers that reside within the physical realms, they begin to no longer hold you into the realm of density. You begin to access what has always been present; your I AM Self.

Your soul seeks voice. There is purpose in your presence. If you feel the pull to be aligned with your divine nature, move into action to embody your divinity. Be inspired by resonance. Do you feel the alchemical, catalytic, potent qualities you already possess? And what now becomes possible?

Today we leave you with the consideration to connect with your deepest knowing. What is it within you that seeks expression? What have you dared not speak? That is the voice of your soul. What becomes possible as your divinity is in action?

Beloved, we hold you in grace as you still and listen to the wind through the trees, for the voice that is your own.

DAY 233: BEYOND ALL EVIDENCE

The process of enlightenment is one that works beyond evidence of its occurrence. The actions of light are not evidence based from the physical perspective. Today, we gather with your Scribe in a busy waterfront square. The beauty of the area is stunning. As people gather and move through this area, what is it they notice? Flowers, buildings, the scenery, the warmth of the day? And yet here we are, in divine collaboration. The only evidence of our conversation is the words upon this screen. Yet the expression of the divine is everywhere.

Living from the physical perspective is dependent upon physical cues. The concept of evidence stems from a physical viewpoint. As your Scribe was growing up there was the experience of an internal chasm. One aspect engaged light, as knowing and connection with her "Council," and one engaged the physical realm of her family that was based upon physical events. A chasm was experienced, as there was no mirror in her life that explained what could not be seen. There was no-thing she could point to and say, "What was that?" For Darlene the journey of enlightenment is the process of honoring that for which there is no apparent evidence. Such is the gift of the journey of enlightenment. The process of acknowledging, honoring, and beginning to understand that which is natural and ever present is an art.

Once you begin to see beyond the physical limitations and the mind's need for confirmation, you are able then to connect with "the good stuff." Your soul's voice is not always one that taps you on the shoulder and says, "Let's go have coffee and talk." It is in the quiet moments of the inner awareness that enlightenment is present. The balance between the physical reality of density and realities coexisting in light is one that is achieved beyond evidence.

There are moments where the internal resonance is so strong, and you are steered beyond the physical distractions of life. Gradually as more truth is revealed, you see from a new infinite perspective that enhances each moment. You see the interconnectedness of All. You see your divine expression and the reflection of the divine in everyone around you.

The bells in the square do not just tell time; the carillon tolls for Love.

DAY 234: LOVE AS YOUR BEACON

Enlightenment is the aligning with Love. It is Love that determines your course. You as Love innately recognize the presence of Love, beyond the understanding and beliefs held in the physical realm. Love's call will be heard by your essence.

The sacred oath of Love is to reach you, returning you to your highest divine expression. In those moments of confusion, of loss, of sadness, grief, and worry, you are seen and held in the comfort of Love's embrace. You, as the guardians of Love, came to this life for the purpose of returning Love, freedom, and peace, through your unique expression. Your divine design holds the keys for the return of Love's promise.

Throughout your day's moments allow Love to lead you, shining the light for your next steps. Look for the resonance that is the indicator you are on the right track. As you allow resonance to lead you, the energy spent on planning, mapping, calculating your life's path becomes moot. It is when you are living in the Now moment that you receive the highest-frequency inspiration. Planning takes a back seat to the guidance, synchronicities, and divine positioning that is possible only Now, as the footprints of Love in action.

Present within our words is a frequency in support of aligning your awareness with your essential truth made manifest. Sense the expression between the words.

Allow Love to lead you. This is a new era. Your soul's voice is seated in Love's Now moment. The old templates of success belong to an old paradigm. Your greatest success, in all planes of your expression, is in the Now.

Day 235: Allowing the Sacred

As you give voice to your divine nature you also invite the sacred expression of the most holy. YOU are the holy of holies. For most, from the perspective of physical reality, days develop a neutral type of normalcy. We invite you to see that what you are doing within the enlightenment process is rare. Many are called, yet few answer. This is available for all beings. Yet you answer Love's call. You recognize the resonance of truth as it unfolds before you. You answer the yearning of your soul's mission for conscious contribution. You have moved beyond, in hearing what is not heard by most. You see what is not seen by most. You remember what is not remembered by most. The light you hold is the emanation of Source.

Moments of beauty capture your attention now. Moments of synchronicity are no longer happy accidents. You see the divine order as it is displayed in front of you. From the vast perspective and experience you bring your immaculate presence. Do you see you are moved to events and moments on purpose? Do you see the contribution you BE? As the divine expression of Love, your awareness has expanded to yet another echelon.

You notice the number of words is no longer our intention. The frequencies held within and behind the words hold the message, the infusion of Love's light and a new language to be remembered.

Day 236: Landmarks in Light

You, as a sovereign expression of the divine, are at choice in every Now moment. When you are informed through your I AM presence, there is a series of evolutionary "landmarks" that are experienced in light that translate to action and awareness in form. Just as there are physical landmarks of maturation, so there are landmarks in light that indicate evolutionary stages of conscious awareness on the way to direct alignment between your human nature and your divine nature. It is the lifting of the veil of separation and illusion.

Today's message is one of remembering that which you came here for, each in your own perfectly timed process. You see the shift already in your physical interactions. The expansion in light is informing your day's experiences. You settle into the solace and remembrance ever present within Love.

As the caterpillar transforms into a new expression, it is not unlike your process of expansion. Understanding that this process is literally transformative opens space for the transformation to occur. The landmarks in light translate to new ways of being in your days. As you release the density of collective consciousness you are able then to embrace the light expression that is uniquely yours. Your journey is not one of the "majority." Your journey is the journey of Love, expressed at the highest levels, as contribution to All.

As you move through the expressions of light and form that are inherently your truth, your experience becomes less understood by most. This is a landmark of having left the boundaries of collective consciousness to embrace your wholeness. Your touchstones now are not from familiar physical cues, but rather from the cues received in light that in turn cascade into form as affirmation of your divine access. Those moments of breathtaking beauty hold within them the resonance of truth. Your experience of joy, freedom, and Love inform your creations, revealing more of the majesty of the sacred. Every leaf, every songbird's melody, contributes to and reflects your divine access.

You live beyond "normal" to the exalted. What now becomes possible? It is in Love and deep reverence that we honor your choices for living your sacred I AM Self. We witness your most holy transformation and the ripples of Love's healing throughout the multiverse.

DAY 237: AMPLIFICATION

The core of today's message is the amplification of your internal connections with your I AM presence in establishing the clarity needed as you integrate your human nature with your divine nature.

In amplifying your most sacred expression, there is yet another layer of interference obscuring your clarity. Early on in the establishment of humanity there were controlling groups that placed upon the inhabitants of the planet Earth limitations and barriers to their own knowing of their divine and empowered truth. Currently, in the expansion of consciousness upon the planet Earth and throughout the multiverse, the reestablishment of divine sovereignty is key. Today's contribution is led by Councils and governing bodies in light that reclaim sovereign reality for All, making possible full divine conscious connection. As the old binds of control are released your path to clarity and full divine expression is unhindered allowing amplification of divine design. Also present are Jeshua, Mary Magdalene, Sanat Kumara, Isis, Archangel Michael, Archangel Gabriel, Legions of Light, the Hathors, Melchizadek, Metatron, Golden Stargate, Infinite Oneness, and Council of the Golden Heart.

As you have released the restrictions and bonds of unconsciousness, the opportunity available in this moment is action that enables the amplification of your divine connection. Remember, this is not a connection that is being made newly; it is one whose pathway is being cleared. You are at choice in every moment. If you choose to connect unhindered with your I AM Self, you will also be connecting with more clarity with the voice of your essential expression.

The veil of illusion has been the curtain hiding the truth of your freedom to express from your authentic nature. Today we have the opportunity to, with the action of Golden Stargate, to release the seals of restriction. As bonds of restriction are released, your own divine light codes within your DNA are activated and catalyzed into expression as is optimal for you.

Golden Stargate 1

If you choose to participate in the action of this Golden Stargate, it is available for you in this Now moment. If not, that choice is also honored.

Please bring all parts of you to be present in this Now moment. Feel yourself sitting quietly, feel the establishment around you within your environment of preparation. As the Stargate opens there is a natural, refreshing experience of communion with your divine expression. Unhindered, the separation between light and form is released. Sit quietly, allowing the gentle connections to be established. Through your crown chakra you may feel activity; a sense of new wiring or a new weaving of connection. This action will continue until it is complete for you.

The access made possible today is again available through the release of limitation and restrictions. Like a vine that has grown out of control and has wound around the rose bush, impacting its vitality, today, the vine is released, allowing your divine expression to shine unhindered.

When the actions of Golden Stargate 1 are complete, move to Golden Stargate 2 (Day 238). Trust the immediate and complete action of this exchange.

As you continue to step back and view your experience from an ever-widening perspective, you see history and limitations newly. The choice to move through them, revealing the brilliance of your divine expression, is yours. We as your divine team support all choices you make in the expression of Love. We support your sovereign right to express freely.

DAY 238: THE WINDS OF
TRANSFORMATION

Today's conversation is a continuation of the action of yesterday's Golden Stargate. It is the direction of the Guardians of Sovereignty that align with the intention you hold of your divine expression made manifest upon the Earth. You may ask what this process has to do with your expanding awareness in light. Those stepping to the forefront of this conversation today include Star Light Guardian Command, Golden Stargate, Jeshua, Infinite Oneness, Mary Magdalene, Isis, Melchizadek, Metatron, St. Germain, Archangel Michael, and Archangel Gabriel.

The expansive expression available for you currently is unprecedented. This window of alignment allows opportunity for restoring the balance of divine masculine and divine feminine within the framework of unity consciousness. Your experience thus far as living the physical experience is skewed by actions of history. The consciousness dawning is unity consciousness. Within the expression of unity consciousness is the opportunity for all to create, unhindered by external interference. As you choose to live beyond the illusory veil of unconsciousness, you open to the vast perspective that has contained limitations imposed by controlling forces. The process yesterday of releasing previously binding seals was available because of your collective choice and actions in consciousness that in turn hold a velocity of creation. The Guardian Command was gathered in the restoration of free will beyond compromise. As your vision sees beyond limitations of form you have opportunity to claim your full divine expression sourced by Love. While perhaps being perceived by your human nature as daunting, you cannot release or heal what you do not know.

The global reach of unconscious action is altered in the establishment of conscious creation from the perspective of enlightenment. A potent force for Love is created through your actions, combined with the actions of many other enlightened ones on the planet Earth.

Golden Stargate 2

The action available today is a completion of that which was started yesterday (Day 237). This Golden Stargate acts in two stages; begin with Golden Stargate 1. Golden Stargate 2 on its own is not complete.

Sit comfortably and watch as your breath slows gently. Feel the infusion of light that is yours. There is an integration in place allowing the smooth and seamless infusion of the full consciousness that is yours, unhindered. The action of this is unprecedented in this format. We acknowledge your divine expression and the intention for your missions of Love. The process of enlightenment unhindered is an extraordinary discovery.

When complete, return to your physical awareness, rested and relaxed in the knowing of your wholeness.

The effect of your actions in the name of Love ripple throughout creation. The light you hold frees those held in the darkness of unconscious existence.

We thank you for your commitment to LOVE.

We remain,

In Service to Love

DAY 239: FREE

In the absence of constraints, we ask, "Now what?" As you settle into the experience of freedom in the absence of constraints previously placed upon your conscious awareness, a new experience arises. Within the new experience, there are possibilities and potential not previously accessible.

From the perspective of the Now immaculate moment, creation holds its greatest potency. As you bring your essential Self to the Now moment with intention, a chain of events is catalyzed. The more clearly you are aligned with your divine expression, the more your creations reflect the vast awareness, frequency, and multidimensional presence of your authentic nature. As you are aligned with your highest expression, your days become the canvas upon which your authentic Self may create.

In the absence of restraints held previously, a new freedom becomes your environment. The experience of containment is gone as the diffuse experience of your divine light moves into your awareness. We ask you to consider the possibilities available as you rest into a new field of awareness. Notice your new experience of freedom. Notice your connection with eternal rhythms. Affirm in those moments that you are experiencing your infinite divine nature.

Mastery in Creation
Hold the vision of a creation as already happened.
When you hold the space of already having achieved something that you wish to create, you in fact draw upon your unlimited resources to make it so. There

is a time lag as the creation is moving through the dimensional realities *toward you. From your space of mastery you may create with clarity.*

Utilize affirmations from high-frequency states.

Remember, the frequency of the creation is a match for the frequency you are in when the creation is first expressed. Utilize affirmations when you are in a high-frequency state of joy, peace, Love, and connection. Develop affirmations that hold a resonance with you. If it is a lie, you will notice your energetic field will experience resistance or a flat feeling.

Instead of creating when you are upset, in low frequency or reaction, identify the state as fleeting and focus instead on your wholeness. Even if you may not be able to feel your wholeness in the moment, realize that your intention for wholeness starts to shift your experience. Then choose to align with your divine nature beyond circumstance.

Notice whether you are limiting your own freedom out of habit. Notice whether you double down on control as a reflex. You have the option of choosing newly each moment.

Who I am is Source extended in form.
I am informed by my highest expression whether I feel it or not.
I choose clarity. I choose Love, I choose joy, I choose delight, I choose peace.
What would Love do?

The precedent set by this body of work is forging new pathways for Love's light to shine and transform creation. With each step you take into the expression of your divine design, your contribution is felt throughout the multiverse.

What now is possible?

We remain,

In Service to Love

DAY 240: CHANGING WHO YOU THINK YOU ARE

As you examine your thoughts and actions through the lens of expanding awareness, you begin to see what had not been available previously. The ability to see what is newly accessible requires an equally expanding perspective. You hold conscious access now to a larger part of your being that resides beyond the material world. This requires not only awareness of this reality but a new perspective from which to assess everything. You are invited to take on a larger perspective, one that is greater than that which you have previously held for yourself. There are no limitations that are inherent within your divine design. Your view of who you are must align with what is possible as you begin to move more freely within living the reality of your divine nature.

As your awareness expands, the ways in which you see yourself and the realities around you shift. From the perspective of your "denser" or known physical expression, the experience in realms of light—the languages, subtleties, and nuances therein—are foreign. Do you see that the way you have viewed your world previously must shift in reflection of the new expansive awareness you hold? We invite you to stand now at the expression of you who resides solely in light; from that perspective you may see more accurately. Perspective determines outcome. For example, imagine yourself at the age of five, beginning your schooling. Your perspective only holds the ability to assess from a five-year-old level. Now shift your thoughts to you, graduated from college, sixteen years later. Now you have the perspective for all the years prior. We use this as a demonstration to search for a new, fine-tuned awareness that acknowledges your expression in light and your energetic expansion. So what used to be very subtle, now, from a more fine-tuned awareness, holds the ability to reflect depth, dimensionality, and light beyond expression of words. Look now for the concepts you hold.

Look to instances of inspiration. When you find yourself in one of those profound experiences, realize in the moment you are experiencing that which is sourced by your highest expression. And look more deeply. Rather than being surprised by what shows up, allow that which shows up to be the new language you speak. Raise your frequency and look for a new way to grasp what is being communicated. The way thoughts are relayed from your expression in light to the you in form has new qualities that communicate depth beyond the spoken word. It truly is a new language. The language of light. You are fluent in it, by the way. When you hear the language of light or see the symbology, automatically look to "absorb" the concept in total. This is much more efficient than the spoken word. Connect with the guidance you have around you, your Council of Light. Allow a new connection to be realized. Expect it. It is the way of the expanded consciousness. Your awareness is now beyond the limitations and barriers that have been the hallmark of experience in the material world. With an expanding awareness it becomes clear you are not alone and never have been. Ask for clarity in connection with the divine support around you.

As you BE willing to see your reality with more depth, you will be met with the new broad band of information, sensing, and knowing.

DAY 241: MERGING WITH YOUR POTENTIAL

As you expand your awareness into the finer expressions in light, the potential you hold is made available for manifestation. You have always had access to that which is your potential. We speak of the manifestation that now is possible as limitations and restrictions are removed and continue to "peel away" from your energetic field of expression. The more you connect with your divine essence the more your human nature must expand to stay aligned with your potential. Those present in light this evening beckon your awareness beyond the limits of perceived possibility to the expansive field of potential held within your divine design. We, as your Divine Team in Light, ask, "What happens if you think bigger than you ever have? What happens if your thoughts are no longer within the bounds of what you would have perceived as normal?" Your field of potential is then accessed. Enlightenment is not something that happens to you. You BE it.

Beyond the realms of what has seemed normal and certainly beyond the collective consciousness accessed by most is the very unreasonable, illogical, field of potential. The words *unreasonable* and *illogical* are descriptions given by your mind for those things that are beyond the world of collective perceived "reality." If you hold to a limited view of reality, how can you connect with your multidimensional expression? Your view of what you think is normal will need to shift to match the ethereal, nonlinear, light-based, quantum creative aspect of your divine design.

Create from Your Field of Potential

Today we ask you to consider "thinking big." And then bigger. And bigger than that! You are tapping into the creative potential you hold as your authentic nature. We ask you to consider creating a large goal. Consider using a large goal, as opposed to a small one, to "test" the system. Within the perspective of "testing," you encounter your limitations and therefore you are not stepping into your unlimited nature. Stay in the field of potential, in the Now moment, and follow your inner resonance. We ask you to consider not a goal that you know is impossible, but one that is free of your own judgments. Just for the fun of it. The goal should hold an affirming quality, perhaps one that really aligns with something you have always wanted to do but haven't found practical. Allow the doorways to open for you out of your expanded way of BEING. BE Love, BE your authentic expression.

Create your goal. Feel the emotional resonance of the goal. Then, from the Now moment, follow your inner resonance. You are not creating a to-do list to get this done. You are being your authentic Self during your day's moments. You are connecting with the magic that is contained within the Now immaculate moment. You are no longer running your life based upon memories. You are present in the magnificence of NOW and hold the door open to usher in your greatest creations.

What is it you need to release in order to embrace your unlimited capacities?

Begin to feel the vibration of your creative pulse. Sync up with the resonance that connects your heart and your creations. Move into action when you feel inspiration. Allow resonance to guide your steps into the unknown. The view from Now is breathtaking.

We remain In Service to Love.

Day 242: The Gates of Heaven

As you step into the grandeur of your divine nature integrated with your physical expression, your reality shifts beyond your wildest imaginings. You have a sense of being comfortable in your own skin and finally "at home." You incarnated for a purpose; we meet in answer to your call. Our work together, our divine collaboration, buoys your expanding awareness, led by your choice and presence in the Now moment. From the spark of creation, within the Now moment, your soul's desires may be manifest. The reality you access is the rarefied air beyond the limitations of physical density. The light you hold reflects your divine access. In these last few days of *In Service to Love Book 2: Love Elevated,* we hold open the gates to your next space of expansion if you so choose.

Those of us in light meet in the unison of our missions of Love, sovereignty, peace, and the entrance into the Golden Age. The new era we speak of is the full-on expression of unity consciousness, where all hear the tolling bells of Love. As you reach deeper into the realms of your light expression, you open the gates of heaven. You are carried on the wings of angels.

What was once thought impossible becomes possible through your declaration. Your emanations of Love radiate throughout creation, making possible the healing of what was not-Love.

Your creations from the space of the immaculate Now moment, fueled by your highest expression, hold an alchemical resonance. Your presence aligns, your presence restores, your presence entrains those around you to a higher frequency. Your sheer presence transforms when you BE you.

We ask you to consider your creations from a grand scale. From the perspective of your divine expression, what is too big? Look for the resonance within to find your next steps. Your reality is now informed from inner direction, no longer from external direction. When you live from the "inside out," your brilliance is not held back in order to not shine too brightly. Your light need not be dimmed to please others. The healing warmth of your light is a catalyst for others who recognize the truth you emanate and begin to remember possibility in their own soul's voice.

These next days are an acknowledgement for your expansion of awareness. We greet you eye to eye, peer to peer, and divine to divine. What within your soul's voice seeks expression?

DAY 243: DEFINED BY LOVE

In the expansion of your awareness, your perspective shifts beyond the definition of the things that are landmarks of the physical realm. You begin to be defined by Love. As you release the barriers to your highest expression, your highest expression is allowed the space to Be within the flow of evolving awareness. If you are not defined by the physical titles, jobs, and events of your life, then who are you? Those present this evening embrace you in the warmth of Love, reflecting the strength, the bold expression of your uniqueness, and the depth of your heart's mission.

If you are not the definitions of the physical realm, then who are you? The limitations of the physical realm no longer are large enough to hold the magnificence and eternal expression of Love that you are. The details of the physical realm, once barriers, limitations, and the sides of the birdcage that held you, are gone. Your vast perspective reveals a whole new reality. Unable to fit within the definitions bound by the physical realm, the new discoveries feel foreign, albeit free of restrictions.

As you glide effortlessly upon the gradient scale of light expression, you feel at home in light. And you know the games of the physical as well. But somehow now the dance of the physical experience is seen for the larger purpose it provides. You see the rich tapestry of creation that is grist for the mill, in the expansion of your soul's conscious expression.

You begin to see the rich expanse of creation with new eyes. Your soul's mission urges you to your greatest creations. The expression you hold is of Love. Through eyes and vision that is only yours, you touch not only the immediate physical realm of your life, but you impact the corners of creation. When you take the wheel of your soul's journey, you begin to create from the highest, most exalted levels of being. You are defined by Love, and it is only Love that your actions define. Your vast expression embodies the connectedness of All.

The sacredness of being inhabits every inhale, exhale, and universe between. Beyond the expression of heaven on earth, you embody Love. Love is All.

DAY 244: GRACE

Good afternoon, dearest Beloveds. It is I, Thoth, moving to the forefront of this divine conversation taking place within this Now immaculate moment. When you engage your divine access, your moments are guided, led, and informed by your highest expression. That part of you which resides in light, by universal law, paves a path of clarity and connection conducted by your alignment. The divine expression holds the presence of Grace. Witnessed beyond conscious alignment, Grace catalyzes the soul's expression and action into form. In a moment of divine Grace, you are transformed. The density of beliefs and experience is altered in the presence of Grace.

It is I, Grace, that is moving to the forefront of this conversation at this moment. Not an entity, but an expression of Love just the same, I AM the wind that moves through creation in the service to Love. I act as Love's liaison, restoring Love's memory of eternal life. From the densest of experiences in the physical reality, the ephemeral experience of Grace halts the moment. From the Now immaculate moment, the presence of Grace brings a break in the illusory veil of reality. For those moments, Love's unconditional essence is in embrace. From the perspective of Grace, each being is met at its utmost essential nature of sacred expression. Grace is available to All. Where there is the slightest opening to the light of truth, I Am there. Where there is despair and the loss of hope, I am there. There, at the point of transition, I am there also, to ease the troubled soul, in restoration of Love's finest expression. Grace does not have a body in the physical realm, yet is seen through the moments of exquisite beauty throughout creation. At the turn of the seasons, Grace shines light on the eternal nature of reality as the bloom bursts through the barren cold of winter.

The message of Grace is the eternal nature of you. The eternal nature of All. As creation evolves, there are constants of Love and Grace. I am with you as you seek your truth. As you look for the openings in your reality that lead the way to the sacred voice of your soul, I, as Love's handmaiden, hold the mirror to your beloved face, revealing your magnificence.

This is Thoth, stepping to the forefront at this moment. Those present in light today usher you into a new, grander expression of you. What does this mean? It means the experience of your authentic nature is more easily seen. It means the joy, freedom, Love, and abundance of your sacred birthright are at hand. You, as seekers of truth, shall find the truth you seek.

The expansion of your awareness into your light expression brings possibility in potential realized. Your divine presence consciously sets a precedent with each enlightened step you take upon Gaia. No longer anonymous, you are seen as the exquisite, unique impulse of creation in service to Love that is your truth.

As you follow the joy of your heart, you fulfill your soul's mission. It is with great joy and delight we meet you In Service to Love.

In Love,

With Love,

From Love,

The Council of Light

In Service to Love Book 1: Love Remembered, Days 1–122
In Service to Love Book 2: Love Elevated, Days 123–244
In Service to Love Book 3: Love Now, Days 245–366

Visit the author online at www.darlenegreenauthor.com or www.thedivineremembering.com

Made in USA - North Chelmsford, MA
1084691_9781949003642
04.22.2020 2015